Influence Human Behavior

The Ultimate Guide to Learning the New Science Driving the Big Change, How to Win Friends and Influence People in Private Life and at Work without Authority

Table of Contents

Chapter 4: Using Humor in Persuasion

Chapter 5: Persuasive Listening to Influence Human Behavior

Chapter 11: Influence and Leading Without Authority

indirect, which are incurred as a result of the use of information contained within this document, including, but not limited to, — errors, omissions, or inaccuracies.

Introduction

Congratulations on purchasing Influence *Human Behavior: The Ultimate Guide to Learning the New Science Driving the Big Change How to Win Friends and Influence People in Private Life and at Work without Authority* and thank you for doing so. The following chapters will discuss the processes the reader can follow to influence the behavior of other people around him or her as well as how he or she can win friends and lead people in different areas of life without authority.

The first chapter is about the main elements an individual needs to be familiar with if he or she wants to influence human behavior. The chapter explains the meanings and differences between manipulation, coercion, persuasion, and influence. From the chapter, you will discover the reason why you should only use two of them and avoid the other two.

The second chapter is about the six Principles of persuasion. The chapter explains the rule of reciprocity, the concept of scarcity, and the principle of authority. The second half of the chapter discusses the principle of consistency, the principle of liking, and the principle of consensus.

The third chapter is about the techniques an individual can use to persuade others. In this chapter, the reader will get insights into the process of putting his or her audience at ease, establishing a rapport with others, and the value of showing vulnerability.

Humor is a great way to establish a connection with an individual or a group and it is a key element in influencing human behavior. Chapter four is about the role of humor in persuasion and the importance of making it relevant in the conversation. The chapter also explains the advantages of humor, its benefit in persuasion, and its connection to smiling and irony.

Chapter five is about persuasive listening and how an individual can influence others through listening. The chapter begins with a lesson on how an individual can develop great listening skills, how people can improve their attention skills, and the process of connecting with people. The chapter ends with an explanation of the Chameleon effect.

Chapter six is about winning friends and how persuasion can help an individual to win friends. Furthermore, the chapter explains how an individual can interest people and the process of winning people through your style of thinking. The chapter concludes with tips on how people can influence others positively without necessarily manipulating them.

Chapter seven is about becoming good at holding conversations, the process of beginning them, and the importance of active listening in conversations. Chapter eight is about body language, types of non-verbal communication, and the process of maintaining positive body language.

Chapter nine is about the development of emotional awareness. The chapter is an in-depth explanation of the steps an individual can take to develop emotional awareness by developing qualities such as self-awareness, social awareness, self-confidence, and relationship management, among others. Chapter ten is a guide for an individual towards becoming more likable.

Chapter eleven is about leadership and influence without necessarily having authority. The chapter explains the process of achieving such leadership and the different types of influences. The last chapter is about storytelling as a way of influencing people.

There are plenty of books on this subject on the market, thanks again for choosing this one! Every effort was made to ensure it is full of as much useful information as possible; please enjoy!

Chapter 1: Understanding Basic Terms in Influencing Human Behavior

Human behavior is a complex process that incorporates various factors that influence how a person acts in a given situation. These factors determine how we react in response to others while also establishing how others respond to us. People conduct and respond almost instantaneously or automatically in different circumstances. However, there is a lot of thought process that made them behave as they did.

The factors that affected and determined the action that a person does are manipulation, coercion, persuasion, and influence. Understanding the differences between these thought processes and their effects could help you to know how and why human beings behave as they do. It enables you also to strengthen your character and improve your insight about people. The knowledge assists you to take advantage of beneficial authority like persuasion and influence while avoiding the traps of manipulation and coercion.

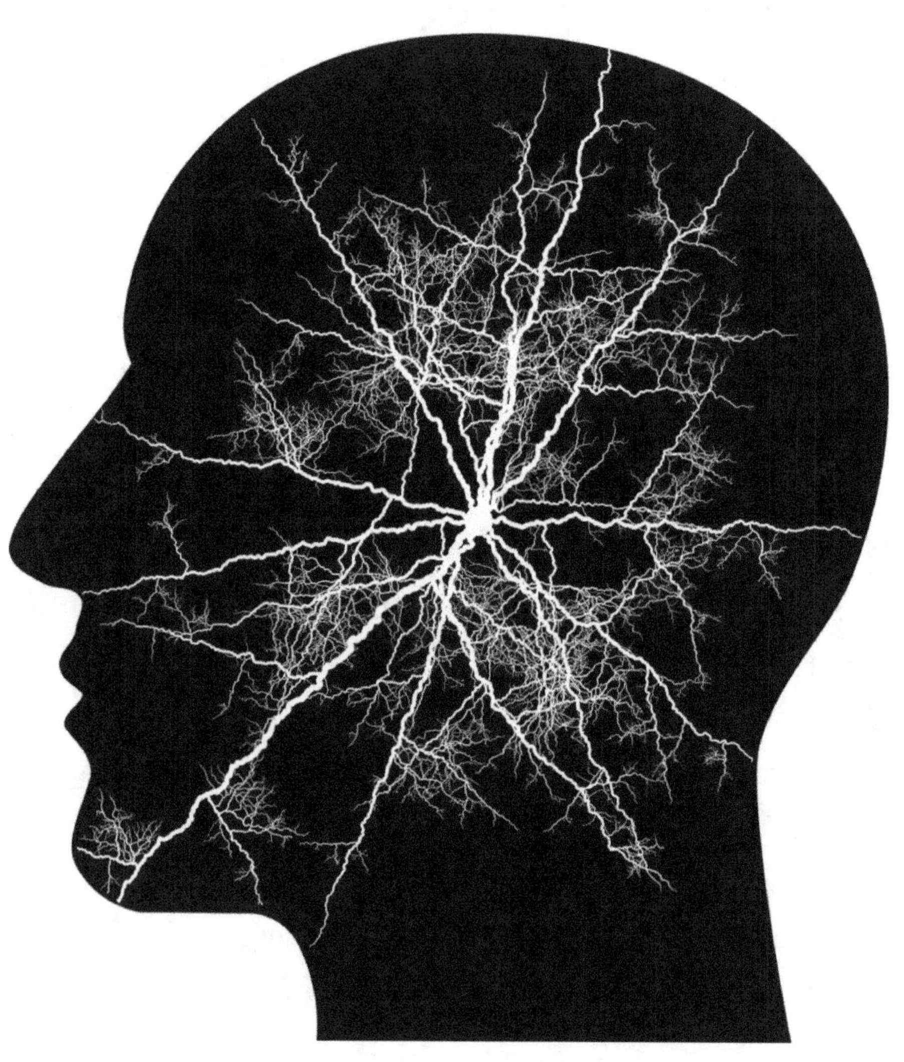

Difference Between Manipulation, Coercion, Persuasion, and Influence

Manipulation, coercion, persuasion, and sway are all terminologies that describe various aspects of human behavior. Understanding their meaning as well as how they function is essential in comprehending human behavior. It can help a person to identify a particular behavior that they exhibit or experience from those around them. The knowledge will allow them to know which conducts they can adapt or improve, and which ones to be cautious about in influencing behavior.

Manipulation

Manipulation seeks to change the actions or attitudes of other people using skillfully deceptive and indirect tactics; it aims to obtain control and power over the victims by distorting their minds and exploiting them emotionally. Positive behavioral influences take place with the intent of establishing and continuing constructive relationships; however, manipulation aims for a person to benefit at the expense of the victim. Manipulative people use certain tricks and deceitful strategies to coerce others into acting or making decisions that they want. These decisions and behaviors benefit the manipulator but are highly detrimental to the victim of manipulation. They experience emotional and psychological damage or pain due to the effects of manipulation.

Manipulators use various means to ensure that they get what they want. They overwhelm a victim with statistics and facts and do not give them enough time to think through a matter before making a decision carefully. They put down the victim by embarrassing them or making statements that target someone's self-esteem as well as use their weaknesses against them. The manipulator also alters facts to suit their agenda. They also like to act as victims by exaggerating their problems as well as making the victims feel guilty over situations that are beyond their control. Additionally, they can pretend not to know what someone is talking about and make that individual do what their responsibility was.

A person must understand manipulation and the tactics that an individual uses to make others act in a certain way using underhanded means. Some people are very skillful manipulators, where they can control others without their knowledge. Someone who understands how manipulation works can protect themselves from manipulative people or situations. They can also learn to control themselves and stop when they feel that they are about to manipulate others around them.

Coercion

Coercion involves the use of force or threats on an individual or group of people to make them undertake or refrain from certain activities forcibly. It uses the threat of force, actual power, or a combination of both to elicit conduct that the enforcer wants. Coercion can use social expulsion, psychological pressures, and economic sanctions to ensure that the enforcer gets what they desire. Coercion differs from persuasion in that; it uses force and a threat to ensure a person acts in a certain way or makes particular decisions.

On the other hand, persuasion looks to convince an individual to act in a certain way by using logical arguments that also appeal to their thought process and feelings. A person uses coercion techniques as a means of obtaining dominance and control over other people. Coercion is a tool that many states use in their governance as well as periodically employ them in international relations when dealing with a challenging country.

Coercion is a cynical tactic as it uses force and threats as the tools to force other people to act in a certain way. However, pressure can be necessary for some political situations, which require intensity to ensure the progress and prevention of war. One must apply it correctly and in a controlled manner to obstruct abuse of power by the enforcer. Generally, a person uses coercion as a last resort in influencing human behavior when other techniques such as persuasion and influence do not work.

Persuasion

Persuasion refers to the process of convincing someone to change their perspectives, feelings and conducts about a particular situation or person by using objective statements and arguments. There are six primary principles of persuasion that one must know to understand how persuasion works. This knowledge will enable a person to identify the situations, which require belief as well as their ability to use it to their advantage. The principles are as follows:

1. **Rule of Reciprocity**

   This principle of persuasion follows the practice of doing unto others what you would want them to do unto you. Reciprocity is where a person feels obligated to repay the favor or good deed or service that they received from someone else. They return the support or service they received by treating the person in the same way. It works in that people do good deeds and help others in the hope that they too will receive the same help or kindness when they need it down the line. Some reciprocity actions can be overt, such as a restaurant offering coupons while others are subtle. This rule also helps a person to achieve a goal that they may not have been able to obtain. It makes people cooperate and work together, for the completion of work efficiently and constructive problem-solving.

2. Principle of Authority

In this principle of persuasion, a person will follow the lead and directions of a person whom they consider an expert in a specific field of interest. They believe that the expert is highly knowledgeable in that area and that they will help them to make quick, convenient, and rational decisions. It depends on the credibility and expertise of an individual to exert appropriate influence. One displays their credentials and knowledge to inform others of the authority they hold in a particular field.

They hang their certifications and necessary documents on the walls in their offices, which potential clients can see and study. They also place awards like trophies in display cabinets in their offices. They could also mention their credentials as part of introducing themselves so that the client is well informed about the person with whom they will work. Proper evidence of authority creates a sense of trust, which allows others to believe and follow someone's decision.

3. Principle of Consistency

This principle uses active, public, and voluntary commitments to persuade others to act in a certain way. Active involvement is where a person thinks and makes a decision by himself or herself. They use words, either spoken or written, to make a promise independently, which they ensure to follow through successfully. A person uses public commitment by highlighting openly the vows that someone wrote.

It promotes accountability of the decision-making process which influences others to follow suit and adjust their attitudes or conducts. Voluntary involvement is where a person deliberately and consciously chooses to make an individual decision or act in a specific way. People make active and public decisions willingly without anyone forcing or threatening them. The deliberate and voluntary choices and actions enable the person to be consistent in fulfilling the promises they made. It also leads to them consistently and steadily allowing others to place more responsibilities on them.

4. Concept of Scarcity

The less available a product is the more desirable and valuable it is to the people. This principle of persuasion uses the law of supply and demand for the scarcity of an item. The concept uses limited offers, restricted access, along with loss language to create a sense of inadequacy.

Restricted access offers people with exclusive access to information, products, or facilities. Loss language uses terms that signal a customer will lose out if they miss purchasing or participating in a particular event. Limited offers comprise time limits as well as a small number of the product on offer. These three features come together to create a sense of scarcity which urges people to respond accordingly.

5. Principle of Consensus

This principle of persuasion uses the idea of safety in numbers, where a person acts after observing the behavior of other people in a similar situation. They copy the feelings and reactions of others who experienced similar circumstances because they initially do not know how to react appropriately. An individual persuades the actions and thoughts of others by referencing the previous behaviors of other people. They could indicate the statistics to show changes due to more people taking specific steps.

6. Liking Principle

This principle states that a person will follow the influence of an individual that they like. A person likes someone similar to them as well as who cooperates and works towards achieving a common goal. They also love those people who pay them compliments. The liking principle bases positive emotions as the factor that makes others follow the lead or directions of someone else.

If a person likes someone, he or she will develop significant and positive sentiments about him or her, which influences their decision-making. They also feel like they can relate to that person of interest, which will make them switch their thoughts and conducts according to the advice or instruction of the individual they like.

Influence

Influence refers to holding the view or conception of the best possible outcome for a business or circumstance, and getting other people to work together to achieve it. Influence does not force nor coerce other individuals into doing an activity of interest. Persuasion uses a short time to bring about results in that; it seeks to convince people to change their attitudes and behaviors. Persuasion strategies aim to sway it in a different direction using arguments that support a particular claim.

In contrast, influence uses the time to earn the sincerity of others in the attempt of making them do certain things. Since impact seeks to win the hearts of the audience, one takes time to ensure that they have gained the sincerity and mindshare of the people of interest. They use this sincerity as a means to inspire and motivate those people to make specific decisions or take a particular course of action.

The basis of influence is the credibility and trust that a person builds over a long period. An individual can influence others by using specific persuasion techniques at the appropriate time. One takes the time to minimize any doubts that others have before they inspire them to make individual decisions. Such a person uses persuasion tactics at the appropriate time to strengthen their influence and solidify the trust that the people have for them. If someone uses persuasion in situations that require powerful tactics, the audience will lose the trust and credibility of that person because the individual comes off as manipulative rather than inspiring. Therefore, influence takes its time to ensure accomplishment, while persuasion is a skill that one can use now without much preamble.

Understanding the basic terms above that associate with behavior will enable an individual to learn the various influences of behavior. The four factors mentioned above are some of the vital means of influencing other people's conduct and attitudes. A person who understands their meaning and usage can be in a position to identify their application in their lives. Such comprehension can assist them to improve their techniques of positive influences such as persuasion. It can also help them to protect themselves and others around them from the negative ones like manipulation and coercion.

Chapter 2: Principles of Persuasion

What do you think of when you hear the word superpowers? Most people think of a superpower as something that exists only in fiction, as is the case with the Avengers or Justice League in the world of comics. However, one can see a particular skill as a superpower if they manage to perfect it. This skill is persuasion.

Jenny Cullen once stated, "I think the power of persuasion would be the greatest superpower of all time." Influence refers to the process of changing another person's convictions or conduct concerning a situation or another individual through sustained reasoning or argument. A person uses logical and organized information to convey their intended meaning. They also employ pathos, ethos, and passion in their message in an attempt to persuade others.

There are six essential principles of persuasion that an individual must know to ensure they can convince other people effectively. Understanding these core principles will enable you to master the art of influence and apply persuasion skills like a superpower in your day-to-day life. This knowledge will also assist you to avoid falling into manipulation from those that may want to influence you negatively.

The Rule of Reciprocity

The first principle of persuasion is the rule of reciprocity. "The basis of social relationships is reciprocity: if you cooperate with others, others will cooperate with you." Caroll Quigley stated this quote because, by nature, people feel obligated to reciprocate the action, service, or gift that they receive from others. This principle relies heavily on what one gives and how they give it.

A person should give out the present or service first and ensures to personalize it to the recipient. They should provide it when the recipient is not anticipating it and present it in a manner that shows sincerity. The recipient will feel the need to repay the act either immediately or later, depending on the situation.

The main idea that one should always follow when applying reciprocity is doing unto others how they would want others to do unto them. Some actions of exchange are apparent such as tactics used by marketers and salespeople while others are shrewder where they use psychological strategies.

For instance, items at a supermarket going for a specific price but have another new thing as a gift if a person purchases it. The company producing and selling that item uses reciprocity in that they hope that by offering the accompanying bonus, the customers will buy more of their things on sale.

Politicians also use this principle in their tenures and campaigns where they use the time and resources that they have while in power to build schools or improve infrastructure. They then use their development projects as a device for getting voters to vote for them. The people will feel that the politician did something to contribute to the development of their society.

One can also apply it at home, where they welcome a new person by holding a party for them. The other person, in turn, will feel the need to return the favor by inviting the individual to an event that they later host. Reciprocity applies in terms of behavior where a person treats others with respect, and they receive respectful responses.

Reciprocity is vital in that it can also enable a person to accomplish something, which they otherwise might never successfully do. They could help a colleague who is in some trouble. In turn, the colleague will assist them in finishing a job if they are unable to complete it, say, due to an illness.

The rule of reciprocity makes someone act in a way that will make others return the courtesy to them and help them when the need arises. Therefore, it plays a massive role in influencing the choices and behaviors of others because of the feelings of obligation that a person experiences when they undergo reciprocity.

The Concept of Scarcity

Scarcity is the second principle of persuasion. This rule applies where people tend to desire more resources that become scarce or uncommon. It uses the laws of supply and demand, where the less available the items are, the more valuable they are to the people. The concept of scarcity uses three features to ensure effective persuasion. It uses limited offers, limited access, and loss language to form a sense of inadequacy.

Restricted offers refer to making offers that have time and supply restrictions, which will influence people to obtain what is on offer. For example, a store has special sale offers on electronics during the Christmas holidays. The advertisements regarding those electronics will mention the special offers and end their marketing with quotes like "buy while stocks last." It gives a message to people that the electronics are few in supply and that there is a time limit in that they are on offer only until the Christmas holidays end. People will buy more of the electronics during the Christmas period than they would have at any other time of the year.

Exclusivity makes the recipients of the limited services feel unique and valued. Exclusiveness provides people with access to restricted services, information, and items. The need or want to feel valued will influence people to buy or acquire the exclusive item or service. For instance, the banking and aviation industries offer VIP services where they treat these customers with high esteem.

In the banks, the customers get the first service and sometimes have their service rooms where they deal privately with the accountants. Airports offer their VIP and first-class passengers their waiting lounges with accompanying refreshments and facilities like access to gaming areas. The first-class cabin on the plane also has different settings in terms of seats and menu, which are distinct from the other economic class offers. The unique access that it offers people makes exclusivity an essential tool for creating scarcity and influencing others.

Loss language refers to implying that a person will lose out rather than profit will strengthen the message that one uses to persuade others. Marketers use loss languages like "don't be left out" to influence customers into purchasing their products. For example, the marketers of a particular play will tell inform customers about the popularity of the show and advise them not to miss the experience by buying their tickets early. An artist can also use the same application when selling tickets to their concerts. Some may even announce retirement and use it to convince others to come and see them perform for potentially the last time.

The concept of scarcity uses these three approaches to exert influence on people's thoughts and actions. Combining all three makes scarcity even stronger, which brings in more persuasion in the conveyed messages.

The Principle of Authority

The third principle of persuasion is that of authority. People are more likely to follow the lead of someone who they consider an expert in a specific area of interest. They use the experts to help them to make sound decisions quickly that they would otherwise spend a lot of time trying to analyze and evaluate.

Thus, the principle of authority relies on the credibility and knowledge of a person in an area. Reliability and expertise are not apparent, and so an individual should always ensure to inform others of their authority. One should use any opportunity that they get to help others to identify and know of their competence. They could display their accomplishments in public, such as having awards in cabinets in the office or hanging certificates on the wall.

For example, a person advises a friend with a weight problem about changing their diet and even recommends the foods to eat. The friend does not follow that advice and instead seeks help from a professional nutritionist. They know that the nutritionist is an expert because they have the certificates and other proofs of authority. The nutritionist suggests the same foods that the initial person suggested, and this friend agrees to follow the recommendation.

The nutritionist had more power than a friend has, which is why their opinion influenced the individual concerned. The display also encompasses items or clothes that symbolize authority such as police uniforms or badges. A person driving a car will stop if a law enforcement officer in uniform waves them down. However, they will likely drive by if the individual stopping them is wearing civilian clothing. The same applies when FBI officers visit someone's home where people agree to talk or invite them into their houses after they show their official badges.

They could also inform others about their skills through short and precise background information. One could mention their experience as a part of introducing themselves. It enables them to give the listener information regarding their expertise as well as establish trust. The listener can rely on their expert opinions to provide them with the best advice regarding the matter of interest.

For instance, a person can state their credentials or have their secretaries mention them when talking to potential clients. If the customer hears that the person has over ten years of experience in that area, they will likely agree to work with that person because the offered mastery persuades them. They can also convey their accomplishments skillfully during casual conversations with others. People network and build connections at official or business events by informing others about their credentials and knowledge adeptly.

One must apply the principle of authority masterfully to be able to have maximum impact and effectively convince others to trust and follow their lead.

The Principle of Consistency

This principle of persuasion uses the influence of active, voluntary, and public commitments to persuade someone. These three commitments come together to ensure that the person executes and fulfills the promise that they made. Active involvement is where an individual decides after thinking it through, and they follow through it to the end. They use written or spoken words to make the decision and that active choice will enable them to see it through to fulfillment.

For instance, a person may want to raise funds for a charity through donations. He or she may make a form in which a person who wants to donate writes his or her name and the potential amount that they will want to give. They then go around the neighborhood, informing the residents about their cause and asking people in each house if they have any interest in the donation. Some will agree to it after hearing about the plan and write their names and the amount they plan on giving. They will donate the amount that they wrote when the time of collection arrives because they actively thought and decided to commit to the cause.

Voluntary commitment refers to a person consciously deciding on his or her own without someone else forcing him or her. Both active and public engagements employ voluntary commitment, as the decisions made are only useful if an individual makes them willingly. The example above shows voluntary commitment as the neighbors choose to engage in the donation project by voluntarily writing their names and the expected donations.

Public commitment is where one makes a promise made by someone public, which boosts accountability among the people. People see that others are participating in an engagement, and this helps them to not only want to join in but also to want to be responsible for their word. The neighbors in the example above will see that other neighbors are writing their names and actively participating in the donation process.

The neighbors who are yet to commit will see the other's commitment, which will influence them also to join. Public involvement increases responsibility. Once the people start to give the promised money, others who do not want others to see them as unreliable will also donate the money they wrote down.

Active, public, and voluntary commitments work together to create a sense of accountability and trust among people. They enable people to behave as they work to ensure that they stick to their words. Agreeing to small commitments also leads to a person accepting similar yet more significant responsibilities since they want to maintain consistency in what they promise to do. Such uniformity thus influences them to make decisions regarding specific promises and fulfilling them in the end.

The Liking Principle

Liking is the fifth principle of persuasion, where a person prefers to follow the ideas of the people that they like. Three factors determine whether an individual is fond of someone else or not. An individual likes a person if he or she pays him or her compliments, if they work together towards mutual goals, and if they are similar to themselves.

If a person pays someone compliments, the complements make the recipient feel good and will be open to that person and have a positive response to their ideas. For instance, when an individual goes to buy clothes, the personnel at the clothes store will pay them compliments as they try out their clothes. The individual will buy as many clothes as possible from that store because of the compliments they received.

If a person works towards accomplishing common goals as someone else, he or she will be receptive and follow the lead of that person. They will feel that they are on the same side and will cooperate to achieve their mutual goals. For example, the detectives use this factor of liking when interrogating a suspect by applying the good cop or villainous cop method.

The suspect will feel that the friendly police are on their side and are working to help them solve the problem. They will cooperate and respond to the good cop. The liking principle influences them to believe that that cop wants to help them solve the case and give them their freedom.

If an individual finds a person who is similar to them, they will make choices swayed by the influence of that person. One is likely to buy something that a friend recommends instead of buying it randomly from the internet or market. They find their friend to resemble himself or herself, and as a result, they trust and follow the choices of their friend.

Similarly, marketers use models that share a similarity with a target audience to ensure effective and productive marketing. For instance, a cosmetics brand uses models of various races to market different skin tones. It provides each person to find a model that he or she can relate to and buy his or her accompanying product.

The liking principle is essential in that a person that an individual likes can have the ability to influence them to act or respond in a particular manner. A person being likable makes someone more recipient to what the individual wants of them affect their decisions and actions

The Principle of Consensus

This is the final principle of persuasion, where a person determines his or her conduct after studying the behaviors of other people. They use signals from other people to decide how they will think, feel, or react in a similar situation. They employ this principle, especially in cases where they initially do not know how to act or react. It persuades them to copy the actions of someone else who is experiencing a similar circumstance.

For example, a person wants to install a particular application on their phone, but they are not familiar with it. They will look at the number of people who downloaded similar applications along with the comments they left. They will then choose the app with the most downloads and positive comments, even though they do not know anything about the app themselves. This principle enables them to feel content with the opinion of the other people who downloaded that app of interest. This consensus leads to the saying that there is safety in numbers since people who are clueless about a situation will look at how the majority of people previously in their shoes reacted or thought.

A person can use the principle of consensus to persuade others by directing them to move with the crowd, where one shows the people what others who are similar to them are doing. Peer pressure works in this case where individuals act like those who share age group with them.

One can also apply this principle by indicating to people an example of how others are already following a specific directive. A manager can persuade other employees to support a new rule if they get a few subordinates to obey the command initially. Similarly, the consensus principle can help one to react appropriately in an emergency. An individual consistently sees posters regarding performing first aid to a person after an accident. The notices also show the statistics that indicate the increased survival rates from previous instances where other people actively reacted.

This individual will likely overcome the trappings of bystander effect when they come across someone who needs first aid treatment. They can also influence the people around them to follow their actions, as they would be setting an example for the others to follow. Thus, companies use statistics from other people's experiences to persuade other people to act similarly. A health institution can use statistics like the one in the example above. An environmental one can use records that show little actions that helped to conserve the environment. An example of this would be people switching off lights in rooms they do not occupy.

The six principles of persuasion can help someone to be an expert at influencing the feelings, thoughts, and behaviors of those around them. It is vital for a person who seeks to change the attitudes or actions of other people to understand the meaning and application of these principles. They should also be in a position where they can recognize when someone is using these principles to persuade them or other people.

Knowing how they work on other people will enable an individual also to realize when people are trying to influence them. They will then know how best to respond. This perception also assists one to avoid adverse effects such as manipulation from others. In conclusion, the principles work to persuade people to make adjustments in feelings and thoughts, which result in minor and significant changes in life.

Chapter 3: How to Be More Persuasive

Persuasion is neither being pushy nor being manipulative. It does not involve constant nagging or the use of force to push people to conform to a certain way. It also does not have the ill intent of manipulation that fools people into doing things that they would not normally do on their own free will.

It borrows a bit from both techniques. It pushes people but in a gentle manner, through tactical ways that are similar to manipulation, but the coaxing does not make or force people to go against their will. Although people tend to think that they come to their own conclusion by processing their thoughts, they mostly arrive at decisions because of other people's persuasive techniques.

Persuasion is a very useful skill to have. Part of the success in life is brought by the ability to sell oneself, one's ideas and one's opinions. People who are able to state their opinions persuasively and their capabilities often end up getting what they want. Such people are able to convince a customer to buy into a product, they are able to convince their boss to give them a salary increment, and they are able to convince a colleague to do a favor for them. Furthermore, they are able to convince their partners to pick up the dry cleaning and are able to convince a toddler to eat something they do not like.

Although some people appear to have the natural ability to persuade others, the art of persuasion is something that everyone can learn and use. It is a very important skill to have in life in various aspects both at home and at work. There are a number of smart ways of making people agree to an idea, listen to an opinion, buy a product or service, give an extra tip, carry out a favor and generally agree to a wish or request. The power to influence people through some of the techniques and advice are here below and can propel you to achieve much more in life than you ever thought of.

Use of Persuasive Techniques

Clever Language

The ability to convince people to buy into an idea first starts with how you present an idea. It involves the kind of language that you use. To be persuasive, you must use clever language. The word "you" gets people's attention. It makes the subject matter relevant to the audience and keeps them attentive. It also speaks directly to the audience, which evokes attention.

Another way of using clever language is to add catchy phrases to a speech as well as phrases that throw people off. Talking about a silver cabbage will attract people's attention rather than talking of green cabbage. The silver cabbage is an element of surprise and is a good step towards catching people's attention and building an unforgettable message.

Positive words and loaded phrases such as "all-natural" can get people to buy into a product. Many advertisers use these phrases because they have a reputation of attracting consumers. The use of imagery also works to give people a good first impression before speaking any words.

Authority

When people use authority figures to deliver a message, they increase their chances of persuasion. People trust authority figures and believe that authority figures are less likely to be wrong. Authority is the reason why businesses use popular bloggers or people with a huge number of social media followers to advertise their products.

Another example of this technique is a person introducing himself or herself as a doctor before pitching the sale of a new drug. By making his or her expertise known, the person is likely to get a better response than a pharmaceutical sales rep who has little knowledge in the medical field. The expertise of the doctor is what people trust and they would be willing to try out the drug because the doctor who has studied medicine knows what he or she is talking about. Likewise, other symbols of authority, such as uniforms and badges, can affect how easily people arrive at a decision.

Liking

People are likely to say 'yes' to people they consider as friends and 'no' to people who are considered as strangers. Given this reason, it is important in business to connect with the customer before pitching a sale. Being friendly to people gives you a good start and goes a long way. Sometimes no matter how good a brand is, people may not succeed at convincing customers to buy from them because of the fact that they have failed to connect with their customers.

People connect more with the persons behind the brand than the brand itself. People also listen to people who are familiar or similar to them as well as people who dish out compliments. What seems like negligible and innocent associations amongst people can greatly influence feelings and decisions. A door attendant, for example, may feel obliged to do a favor for a tenant who always says good morning to him as he leaves for work and asks about his day when he returns in the evening. The same door attendant may refuse to get the door or assist a snobbish tenant with their luggage.

Commitment and Consistency

It is almost impossible to persuade people when you yourself are not interested in what you are selling or pitching. Others can see your commitment to a particular cause or thing and influence others to follow you. Consistency is also equally important as commitment. When you consistently talk to people about a particular thing, eventually you retain their attention.

Another way of using commitment and consistency to your advantage is getting an audience to make commitments towards something and reminding them of their commitment constantly and consistently. Eventually, they have no option but to honor their commitment through your consistent efforts.

Reciprocation

People are more inclined to do a favor for someone who has done something nice for them in the past. People can use this principle in persuasion. When you do something nice for people then ask them to support you in return, they will feel obliged to do that which you request them to do. If you are business, for example, you can offer people free consultations or discounts then when you ask people to come to your premises, they will feel obligated because of the free service that you have rendered to them.

Another good example of the power of reciprocity is tipping. A waiter who offers a gift to his or her customers when they finish their meals is likely to receive a tip than one who does not. If the same waiter also gives an extra mint then the customer will feel obligated to leave a bigger tip than he had planned for. The technique of reciprocity can get people to do smaller favors by first asking them for big favors; when you can ask a person for a big request and they decline, you ask them for a smaller request. The person is likely to say yes to the smaller request because of the compromise you have made of reducing the size of your request.

Social Influence

Human beings are social animals and they tend to follow certain paths just because other people have taken the same path before them. They also have a tendency to follow what other people are doing even if they do not agree with it. Others even follow masses of people blindly and believe that what the other people are doing must be the right thing, which means that they too should join the party.

Businesses use social influence to attract customers; they use testimonials from previous customers to attract new customers. People are likely to buy into a product when they see other people known or not known to them using a product. Social proof also explains the reasons why people begin drinking despite the numerous health concerns and bad taste associated with such habits. It is the number one reason people act in a similar manner as their peers.

Being Scarce

Giving certain services to only subscribers, limiting seats, products, or the duration to access a certain product is also another tactic very useful in persuasion. This tactic of scarcity creates a sense of urgency and prompts a person to take action; otherwise, they risk losing out. Scarcity also uses the principle of supply and demand. When something appears to be in low supply, the demand for it goes up.

If, for example, a person is able to convince people that a certain product is available for a short period of time and in low quantity, then the demand for the product goes up and people are more likely to rush to clear the product's stock. Another example of the technique of scarcity in play is a child getting to her last cookie. He or she will savor and enjoy this last treat because they are about to experience the scarcity of their delicious treat.

Anchoring

Anchoring, for example, in pricing can be a very useful tool for persuasion. Car sales representatives especially, know how to make use of this technique. When a customer wants to purchase a car, they normally quote a higher value for the customer to leave room for the customer to bargain.

For example, if a car is worth $13,000, a sales representative might quote for you $15,000. Any reasonable person will want to bargain the price that he or she gets at first. After lengthy negotiations, both of you will finally agree on $13,000 and both of you will somehow be contempt with the negotiated price. You, as the customer, will feel especially happy because of the $2,000 that you have saved.

What you are probably not aware of is that the initial price of the car was an anchor to try to lure or persuade you into getting the car for its actual value.

What you thought was a good deal turns out to be the real value of the car. This tactic is very popular in business and it gets customers to purchase items without offering them much of a discount.

Putting Your Audience at Ease

Persuasive people have excellent communication skills. They are good listeners; they listen not with the aim of responding but with the aim of understanding what is important to other people. When people believe that people have heard their message, they can concentrate on what another person is saying. Persuasive people also tend to focus on other people instead of themselves.

They always have other people's interests in mind. They do not use words such as "I want" or "I think." They take what they are selling and make it seem like it is something that you need. They explain their suggestions in a way that is of benefit to you. Persuaders also put their audience at ease by maintaining proper eye contact, they do not gaze at a person for too long or hold stare downs. They also show empathy and are open-minded. Persuasive people also remain calm and relaxed no matter what response they encounter.

Establishing a Rapport

For you to be more persuasive you must learn to build rapport with people before anything else. People who greet you and ask about how you are faring before asking for a favor are simply trying to establish a rapport so that you are likely to grant them their request. The same concept works in many other areas whether you want people to buy a product or want them to accept an idea or opinion. How then can people easily establish rapport?

Building a rapport with a person requires you to mirror and match your body language to those you are speaking to. If the person or people use hand gestures, you must also use hand gestures. If they move in a certain way, you should move in the same way. Mirroring body language suggests that you should move your left hand when the person you are speaking moves his or her right hand. However, the key to mirroring is to remain subtle and sincere when copying the other person's movement.

Another way of building rapport is to match your voice to the other party. The tone and volume of your voice are important in how people receive and act upon your message. The pace at which you speak should also match the pace of those you are speaking to. If a person is speaking to you using very low tones, you must follow suit. If he or she is loud, you can also speak loudly.

Showing Vulnerability

The most important aspect of persuasion is establishing a connection with your audience or the people or person you are trying to persuade. One way of getting people to trust you and your credibility is by showing that them that you are vulnerable and thus human. People get disarmed when you tell them of your mistakes.

The moment you start speaking of your failures and of course how you overcame them or what you did to prevent the same mistake from happening a second time you begin to get people's attention. Speaking about your fears also helps people relate better to you. Some may argue that this is a terrible thing to do but showing people that you are human to draw them closer to you is a good idea. Building unity and trust through showing vulnerability is also far much important than the content of what you are presenting to people. Speaking of downfalls is also another way that makes you appear human and believable.

Using Names

Persuasive people are pleasers; they know how to make people happy and feel important. One way they do so is by referring to people by their names. They do not just greet you, leave it at that, they go ahead and ask for your name, and address you by it every time they talk to you. When you refer to someone by their name, you make them feel validated.

Going the extra mile of pointing out where you met or mentioning the last conversation that you had, makes a person feel like they matter because you took the time to register their faces and the encounter that you had. Even if you do not have a good memory, mastering names can be a good brain exercise. Devising creative ways of remembering names can prove to be of benefit later on.

Offering Value

When an individual offers them something of value, people can be easily persuaded. Before you offer people things, it is important to find out what they need or value. You can also make whatever you are offering to appear to be of value by anticipating possible objections.

Before people can even begin to tell you why something does not work for them, you should already have a solution for them. However, sometimes it is important to have confidence in the value of what you are offering and let it sell for itself. Forcing people into something might have the opposite effect. If something is of value to them, it will persuade them, not necessarily the person.

Self-Deprecating

Ironically, self-deprecating people are very confident people. They are fully aware of their weaknesses and shortcomings and know how to use them to their advantage. They are not afraid of pointing out their faults to other people; in fact, they do it openly but in a humorous way. Self-deprecation is also a way of showing that you are vulnerable which as earlier indicated draws people close to you. It also helps people not to take you too seriously especially if you are in a position of authority.

It makes you more approachable by setting aside your superiority and minimizing the difference in status. Self-deprecation also fosters trust. When you reveal to people your shortcomings, you are showing honesty and people tend to appreciate honest people. Honest people give honest opinions and if they say that a certain product is valuable, then chances are that it is truly valuable. Self-deprecation should, however, be used cautiously. You do not want people to think of you as a loser. It should be humorous and if it happens spontaneously the better.

Anecdotes, which are small personal stories can also be used in a self-deprecating manner. However, they have to be short, real, and to the point. Epigrammatic, which are short, informative statements, can also make you appear less of a know it all. An example of a good epigrammatic used to self-deprecate is a saying by Oscar Wilde that states, "I'm not young enough to know everything." People can also use self-deprecating statements to break the ice, especially if they are humorous jokes. They lighten the mood and put both parties at ease.

Part of being good at persuasion is recognizing persuasive techniques that are in use on you. Take a moment to think about some of the reasons why you did something for someone or agreed to something. Chances are one of the above techniques was used to convince you to arrive at doing what you did. You can also undertake this experiment; sit down and open a random television channel and note down the different persuasion techniques in use to convince you to tune into another show, to buy a certain product, to seek a certain service or to visit a certain holiday destination.

By becoming aware of these techniques, you can begin to appreciate and understand the power of persuasion as well as begin to apply it in your life. People achieve persuasion through being knowledgeable and confident about what you are trying to persuade others to take in. The above techniques can help you easily make the conversions that you want but your knowledge and confidence are also important.

Avoiding long pauses and saying words like "Ummm" makes you look unprepared. Using a word like "I" can work to your disadvantage; it detaches you from your audience. Using "we" and "you" is likely to draw the attention that you want. Body language also matters. If you appear nervous and fidget a lot, you may fail to convince people about what you have to offer because their attention will be on how nervous you are instead of the message that you are trying to pass across.

Chapter 4: Using Humor in Persuasion

Persuasion is the process of changing a person's attitude or behavior using logical statements and arguments. Humor can have a significant role in effecting the view changing process of that person. One has to apply it appropriately in a persuasive message to ensure a maximum and desired impact on the target audience.

Have you ever noticed that some advertisements on television have some humor in them? Langston Hughes, who was an American poet, once described it as laughing at what you have not gotten when you ought to have it. A person can use humor to influence someone else's perspective or actions. The key to successfully doing so is to know how to incorporate it fittingly in a persuasive message. The points below indicate how humor functions and how you can use it when trying to persuade others.

Humor Should Be Relevant

A person organizes their knowledge and information in mental memory systems called schemas. They activate the significant schema whenever they think of something. Humor is relevant when one uses it in regard to the body of information and

knowledge that they have. A person should be able to portray the setting of a joke mentally. They should also identify and impede a discrepancy in the various interpretations while maintaining only the funny ones. An individual who applies these will be able to understand the joke and enable others who are listening to be in on the fun they want to impart.

Relevancy comes in when one uses the knowledge of the audience concerning the intention of the persuasive message. A mental connection should exist between the joke and the actual situation or product that someone is addressing. Humor makes people laugh or find amusement, which means that it can cause them to have a good mood. Such good feelings bring in positive responses where the audience becomes more open and willing to follow the message that one is trying to convey. Humor should be unforeseen, in that, the audience establishes the connection of the communication with the information from their schema to mentally connect ideas and interpret the funny meaning. Thus, the more relevant the humor application is, the more influential it is on the audience.

How to Use Humor to Your Advantage

Humor can bring many positive results when a person uses it. The important thing that one needs to understand when using humor is to know when to employ it in their message. Sometimes an individual is funny with witty comments but applying their amusement at the wrong in the wrong way can result in embarrassing, awkward and even offensive situations. So, how can a person use humor appropriately and make the best out of it? Three essential factors help one to employ humor in the best possible ways. Understanding these factors will enable you to use fun to your advantage by assisting you to know when, how and where   to   use   it   appropriately.

A. **Know the Audience** – Finding a joke to be funny or having a sense of humor is subjective. Hence, a person has to combine their knowledge and that of the target audience to ensure everyone can understand the intended fun. Knowing and understanding one's audience enables them to avoid awkward scenarios. They avoid saying jokes, which may offend the audience or those that they do not find to be funny. They should research to find out about the audience's memory schemas. They then learn how they can make a relevant, humorous link between those schemas and the message they are conveying.

B. **Integrating** – One uses humor when they can extract it from the subject matter that they are addressing and consequently applying it relevantly. A person should introduce it at a suitable time and in the appropriate context, which the audience will be able to connect with and understand. For instance, advertisers should use unexpected humor at a proper time in the commercial to ensure the customers will always recall the product. The integration of fun refers to comedic timing, where there is perfect alignment between context and fitting mood.

C. **Expression Style** – One should use simple and direct language to ensure the audience fully comprehends the intended message and accompanying humor. If it involves verbal communication, a person should ensure to use expressive voice in conveying their message and humorous lines, which captivates the audience even further. Humor contained in a passionate message helps the audience to feel the context as though they were relieving it and grasp the mood quickly as well.

The Benefit of Humor in Persuasion

Humor can play an essential part in influencing the attitudes and conduct of other people. A persuasive message with a sense of humor will have a positive impact on the target audience, which in turn will make them more likely to change their opinions accordingly. The following are some of the benefits of using humor in the persuasion process.

A. **Better Health**

They say laughter is the best medicine, and the purpose of humor is to get people to laugh at a situation or themselves. Good fun makes a person laugh, which in turn makes them happy and allows them to be in a good mood and a positive mindset. Positive feelings on the inside translate into positivity on the physical outside. It leads to better health and psychological well-being. Good health gives a person the energy to try out new things. Hence, they are more open to receiving influence from other people.

B. Builds Rapport

Humor helps to build rapport with others and makes people likable. Liking is one of the crucial principles of persuasion where a person is more receptive to someone they like. They will readily listen to and cooperate with those who they see as being likable. Humor thus helps in persuasion by making the people involved to be friendly.

C. Obtaining Concessions

Humor creates a feel-good factor and makes the listener relax and be in a good mood. This good mood enables them to have an open mind and be more likely to listen to suggestions and provide concessions that a person requests. It allows a person to influence the party of interest to make decisions that will lead to the provision of permits along with other requests.

D. Improves Communication

Humor leads to enhanced communication because it captures the attention of an audience. Relevant humor keeps the attention of the audience to the words that a person conveys. This attention enables persuasion to occur with ease and makes the intended message memorable to the listeners. The audience will have a better understanding of the meaning of the intended word is as well as comprehend the need for a change in behavior or perspective.

E. **Relieves Tension**

Humor causes laughter, which helps the person of interest to relax and diffuse any tension that was taking place. For example, if people were getting tense in arguments during business negotiations, appropriately timed humor can help to release that pressure. This relief enables the people involved in the consultation to influence others better and agree to reach a particular conclusion.

F. **Positive Emotions**

Positive emotions lead to a positive mindset. Laughter is a medicine that can turn negative feelings into positive sentiments. A positive person looks at new or different situations, behaviors, or perspectives in a good light. Therefore, they are likely to follow directions that can change their actions and attitudes. Humor creates positive emotions, which make it easier to persuade someone about a particular circumstance or conduct.

G. **Reduces Hostility**

Humor reduces hostility, which impedes a person's reception to persuasion. Humor can enable people to reduce the hatred that they experience and allow them to solve situations. In this case, fun removes the blinding aspect of hatred and helps the people to identify a problem and accept the significant influence that brings about the solution of the issue of interest.

H. Improves Morale

Humor boosts a person's morale because it enables them to laugh at their situation and make fun of themselves. Negative experiences in life are unavoidable and being able to laugh at them can help one to improve their morale in an unfavorable position. The improved confidence can help the person to be more open to switching to using new ideas about dealing with a particular problem or situation.

I. Boosts Brain Power

One needs to be witty and be quick at thinking on their feet to ensure they employ good and relevant humor. Humor thus improves creativity and brainpower, which, in turn, can help one to make better decisions regarding a problem or situation. Humor keeps one's brains active and helps them to be more open to changing their approaches to different circumstances. They are more receptive to persuasion since they can think from different and necessary perspectives.

Smiling is Contagious

People mirror the facial expressions of others in an attempt to understand their feelings. If a person smiles at you, you will find yourself smiling back. Even when a person reads about someone smiling in a book, he or she will also be smiling himself or herself while studying. Smiling is contagious, and it helps a person to try to understand someone else's emotions subconsciously and respond to them appropriately.

Smiling creates good sentiments and makes a person appear friendly. Mimicking a smile also allows an individual to reflect on the positive feelings and make them more receptive to the person smiling at them. It makes it easier to get them to listen to what someone is directing, and they are likely to follow the lead of that person. Hence, a person can use smiling appropriately and tactically to prompt good feelings and positive responses, which enable persuasion to occur.

Irony

The irony is where an individual uses words in a way that the actual meaning of the phrase is different from the intended purpose. The intended meaning is usually the opposite of the exact meaning of the words. One can use irony to persuade others by showing them the irony of their situation or those of others. They use that observation and understanding of the ridicule or mockery to change their minds or behaviors as necessary. There are three types of irony. Understanding them can help someone to know how to apply them when trying to influence the thoughts and actions of others.

A. **Verbal** – A person says words that they do not mean. The meaning of their words is the opposite of the actual meaning of the words that they say. For instance, a person tells someone whom he or she does not like but is in their home, "Wow! How nice of you to visit us."

B. **Situational** – It takes place when a person is not aware of how a situation affecting someone else will affect him or her. They laugh at someone else without knowing that they will soon be going through a similar circumstance. In writing, it refers to a situation where both the characters and the reading audience do not know how the real event will affect them.

C. **Dramatic** – This irony takes place when the characters of a story are not aware of what will happen to them while the reading audience knows of the implications. Humor comes in when the actions of the characters are comedic if one thinks of the connection between their current conduct and their impending misfortune. Dramatic irony can persuade someone by presenting them with the lessons learned from observing the actions and attitudes of the characters   of   interest.

Irony uses its scenarios and meanings to persuade others. It presents lessons regarding behavior and perceptions in particular situations as the means of convincing a person to change their attitude or actions as needed.

Humor is a tool that a person can use in the persuasion process. One needs to understand how humor works concerning the context of interest and appropriate timing. If they apply it correctly and in a relevant situation, then it can become vital in persuading others. It can be a tool for convincing and influencing others to change their thoughts and conducts as necessary.

Chapter 5: Persuasive Listening to Influence Human Behavior

How to Become A Better Listener

Listening is the process of paying attention to other people when they talk. Listening involves hearing what others are saying and understanding the message, they are trying to convey.

Listening consists of three processes:

- Affective - the motivation to listen to other people

- Cognitive - the process of understanding, receiving and interpreting the message being conveyed

- Behavioral - responding to others with feedback

We become better listeners by practicing the following:

1. Keeping eye contact - When we maintain eye contact, we tend to focus more on what the other person is saying and avoid distractions from objects or people around us. When we look around and not at the person speaking, it actually shows that we are not listening.

2. Put any distractive objects away - If you give in to

distractions easily, avoid having objects like phones, tablets, notebooks, and pens near you. When you fiddle with such objects, you forget to pay attention to the person talking. So put away any objects, you do not need them while listening.

3. When listening, just listen - To become a better listener, do not interrupt or jump in with your own suggestions when someone else is talking. Really listen keenly and wait for the speaker to finish, then if they still have not touched on what you wanted to add, then you can offer your suggestion. Avoid working on a reply even before the speaker is finished. When you do so, you destruct yourself from capturing the full information.

4. Be honest about any limitations - If you have a hearing problem, it is important to let the other person know so that they can either come closer or adjust their voice accordingly. If you have been listening to someone for a while and you need to take a break or have something to eat, be honest and tell the other person. This way you can continue the conversation later without trying to fake undivided attention.

5. Listen to learn - To become better listeners practice to listen to learn not to be polite. If you are not learning, then you are pretending to listen. Do not just listen out of generosity strive to learn something.

6. Ask questions - You become a better listener by asking more questions, by using the questions; the speaker is able to explain further any area you did not capture well. Great listeners show curiosity by asking questions.

7. Repeat back what you heard - To become a better listener always tell yourself that you are going to tell someone else about what you have learned. By doing so, you will be more alert and attentive and get the most out of the message conveyed.

8. Observe body language - When listening, it is important to study the other person's body language. If you notice the speaker is nervous or tensed, a good listener will appear relaxed and avoid appearing as confronting. Observe when the speaker's voice and pitch changes, it may mean that they are trying to stress-out an emotion.

9. Have an open mind - When listening, avoid judging or forming opinions about the speaker as soon as they start talking. Have an open mind. Put yourself in their shoes, and ask if it were you there would you want people listening? This will help you become a better listener.

Become an Attentive Listener

Research suggests they we only remember between 25 percent and 50 percent of what we hear. Clearly, we all need to improve our listening skills. Here are some useful tips on how to become an attentive listener.

1. Be an active listener - This involves listening to what someone is saying and understanding the message conveyed by paying attention, being nonjudgmental and non-interrupting. Observe any non-verbal messages that may have a connection to the message.

2. Try engaging emotionally with the speaker - You tend to be more attentive when you connect with the speaker emotionally. If you feel sad about something the speaker expresses, you tend to empathize with them, which makes you pay more attention.

3. Pay attention - to be an attentive listener, you need to give the speaker undivided attention. Maintain eye contact and shut down any distracting thoughts coming your way. Avoid any distractions from the environment. Paying attention includes observing the speaker's body language.

4. Use minimal encouragers - These are actions or words that encourage speakers to express themselves fully. Using verbal words like uh-huh, yeah, mm's, sure, then or non-verbal gestures like nodding your head, smiling, or holding that okay sign contributes towards becoming an attentive listener.

5. Reflect on the message - You can reflect on what the

speaker is saying and ask questions to get clarity on what is not clear. An individual can reflect by repeating and paraphrasing the message to decipher the message. By asking yourself things like "what he is trying to say is that…"

6. Mirroring - Mimicking the speaker's facial expressions, gestures and attitudes is a sign of attentive listening. Replicating what others are saying or doing is a sign that you favor and like the message. When we mimic empathy, it shows that we relate to the speaker.

7. Posture - lean slightly forward while sitting down to improve your chances of becoming an attentive listener. Sometimes slanting your head or resting your head, on one hand, this shows that you are attentive and are paying attention.

8. Avoid interruptions - an attentive listener will always allow the speaker to finish talking, and then ask him or her questions, then allow the speaker to completely explaining each question before responding again. Ensure your responses are in line with the questions, this will show that you understand the message.

9. Not Engaging in Bad Listening Habits - To become an attentive listener, you have to avoid bad listening habits like not showing respect to the speaker, rushing the speaker, daydreaming, ignoring what you do not

understand and asking irrelevant questions.

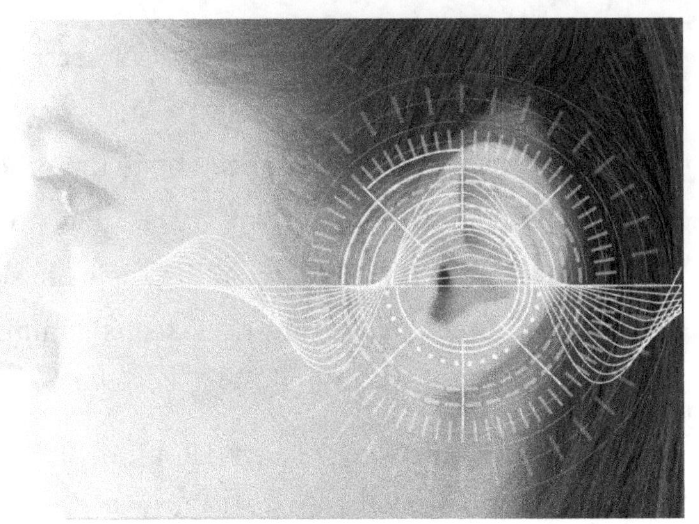

How to Connect with People

1. Find What You Have in Common - When you want to connect with someone, the first step is to look for what you have in common with him or her. Such things may come up during the course of your conversation. Listen keenly and look out for things like which football club they support, favorite food, hobbies which can help you connect. Avoid asking using questions, let it flow naturally when conversing.

2. Make Others Comfortable - When you want to connect with people make, they feel comfortable. Be friendly,

exude positive energy, let down your guard and make them feel at ease when they are around you. Avoid expressing negative body language.

3. Give Compliments - One way to connect with people is to offer sincere compliments. During your conversations, note something you admire about the other person and compliment them. Take care not to overdo the complements or complimenting their physical attributes. A compliment like "that necklace is stunning, where did you get it?" will do the trick.

4. Repeat Something They Mentioned Before - When conversing, you can echo words the other person mentioned before. This shows that you were actually listening and care about what they are saying which builds a connection.

5. Be Open - In order to connect with people, you need to open up to them and be vulnerable so that they can learn a thing or two about you and gauge if they want to connect with you as well. However, you do not have to tell them everything about yourself- just a segment about your life you think they would find interesting.

6. Be Authentic - Connections really work well when we are being our true authentic selves. You tend to connect with people you have things in common with. Therefore, if you are masquerading or pretending to be something or

someone you are not, you have to keep it up every time you meet up with that person which can be overwhelming.

7. Be Thankful - Connections are built on simple things like taking time to really thank people. This makes them feel appreciated. When you thank people for offering a service, it is good to take the time to elaborate on why you are so thankful; this can help you connect with them.

8. Put Names to Faces - When you want to build connections, you have to remember people. It is important to remember people's names. Many people struggle with remembering names, especially in a social setting. However, do your best to remember their names, repeat it internally several times and associated it with some unique feature about that person. People feel acknowledged and important when they are referred to by their name.

9. Be of Value - People appreciate those who offer valuable information or offer referrals that may interest them. For example, if they have an interest in certain recipes, which you have, lend them, or refer them to where they can get them. Offering a service even in small ways is a great way to connect with people.

10. Empathize - Showing that you care about someone is a great way to build deep connections with him or her. When you empathize and show kindness to people you just met, it goes along way.

11. Do Research - If you find it had to connect with people by holding conversations, you can do a little research ahead of time. A little prep work will boost your confidence. Think through questions that will keep conversations flowing.

The Chameleon Effect

The chameleon effect refers to the process of subconsciously mimicking other people's mannerisms, facial expressions, attitudes, and behaviors. It is the process of changing behavior or mannerisms to match those of others in a social setting. For example, the chameleon effect occurs when you adopt the mannerisms of a good friend after you spend a lot of time with him or her or when you take on a French accent after spending time with a family member who lives there.

Mostly people mimic others because it has the potential for increasing their likeability. People respond better to you when they notice you behaving like them. People who get along well behave the same way because they unintentionally mimic each other. This effect is in use in social situations and can take place in everyday interactions with people.

The chameleon effect allows people to think they are similar to others, which in turn can build relationships, making it quite an important social skill. However, the chameleon effect varies from imitation. The difference is that the latter happens consciously while the other occurs subconsciously.

Three experiments to answer the following questions related to this effect include:

1. Do people subconsciously mimic others? - The results for this question showed that people naturally mimic others including those they have just met.

2. When we mimic people, do they like us more? - The results showed that people indeed mimic others to increase liking.

3. Do people with high-perspectives exhibit the chameleon effect more? - The result was that high-perspective takers showed the chameleon effect more than the low-perspective takers.

Occurrence

The chameleon effect occurs subconsciously as people interact and communicate with each other. People tend to imitate attitude, mannerisms, and body postures of those they feel a connection with and have similar interests with.

Downside

People with certain medical conditions like autism may be less likely to use the chameleon effect; this is due to their inability to be aware of the actions of others consciously and subconsciously. Therefore, such people may find it hard to establish connections or rapport with others.

In addition, normal people are less likely to build a rapport with those with such medical conditions because without mimicry they may appear to be unfriendly, not open, and different. These people do not understand non-verbal communication and may find it hard to understand the common cues used in a social setting.

Development

When growing up, parents imitate the baby's expressions while vocalizing the emotion. This imitation helps the baby associate the emotion with the expression. As the baby grows, they express their emotions, gestures, and facial expressions by imitating their parents. This action enables them to develop self-control and self-awareness.

As they grow, the chameleon effect helps people excel in social situations and help individuals create long-lasting relationships.

Power Dynamics

People tend to mimic those people with power or high status. Doing so gives them the deceptive impression of high status and allows them to gain favor with the person in power. On the other hand, mimicry can be useful to people with low status because they can use it to persuade those with privileges to help them. This effect works well in situations like job interviews, promotions, and parent-child interactions.

Chapter 6: How to Win Friends

Friends have a very powerful impact on your life. They contribute to your mental health as well as your well-being. Good friends walk with you through your difficulties and share in your pain and joy. They celebrate with you during the good times and comfort you when you are in despair. Friends also provide you with company, bring happiness, and avert loneliness and isolation.

To show you just how important friends are, studies have shown that lack of friendship results in substance abuse and physical inactivity, which are both not good for your overall health. Another study also shows that having meaningful friendships can give you longevity.

All these benefits seem rewarding but we have to admit one thing; making friends, as you grow older is not as easy as making friends when you were young. However, it is possible to develop deep connections with people and form long life friendships no matter what age you are.

How Influence and Persuasion Can Help to Win Friends

Any person with the ability to influence and persuade people can easily make friends. For a person to be able to persuade people he or she must first try to develop a relationship with the people he or she intends to sway and this relationship is what can grow into a friendship. Some of the techniques used in persuasion also work to enable people to connect with one another and they include:

1. Listening

    For people to form friendships, they must be able to communicate well with one another. Communication involves both talking and listening. Experts advise that people who listen more are better communicators than those who talk all the time and dominate a conversation. Effective communication is critical in persuasion. Persuasion requires that you listen keenly to the needs of the other person so that you can know how to align yourself and ensure that you meet the needs of the person you are conversing with. When you also listen to a person, you are in a way showing concern and care. You are taking time to validate the other person's thoughts and when people feel heard and validated, they can welcome the idea of developing a friendship with a persuasive listener.

2. Giving

Persuasive people are givers rather than takers and they give without expecting anything in return. This technique is very tactful; people like receiving gifts and favors. When a person also receives a gift or favor, they feel obliged to return the favor or give their own gift. This concept of gift-giving is in play among friends and therefore proves that the habit of giving seen in persuasion can also lead to people forming friendships.

3. Liking

People like people who are attractive or similar to them and this principle is often in play when persuading people. Persuasion can convince people that they are alike or similar in a particular way. Since friendships develop out of having a common ground with other people persuading people, using common interests can easily develop into friendship.

4. Showing Vulnerability

Persuasive people know how to use their weaknesses and vulnerabilities to win people over. They admit their shortcomings so that they can get a person to develop trust in their honesty. This technique of showing vulnerabilities can also work in winning friends. Most consider vulnerable people trustworthy and trust is very important among friends.

5. Being Consistent

    You can win over friends by persuading them with your consistent behavior, admirable ideas, and commitment to growing the relationship.

How to Interest People

1. Show excitement - First impressions are very important. The first encounter with someone normally sticks in your mind and makes you develop a perception about a person. Therefore, it is important to come across as jovial and warm when we are interacting with people. Giving that warm energy creates a positive environment where we are able to influence people into a meaningful relationship.

2. Showing interest in the other person - You should aim to listen 75% of the time and leave the remaining 25% for talking and silence People like is to talk about is themselves and the things that they enjoy doing which means that when you give people an opportunity to talk about themselves they will love you for it. You can keep the

person engaged in conversation with you by asking even further questions. Showing sincerity in wanting to know more about a person also goes a long way in strengthening the bond. Letting the other person talk also gives you time to explore the other person's interest and discover what the common ground between the two of you is.

3. Make people feel important - Another way of interesting people is by making them feel important without expecting them to do anything in return. You do not have to go out of your way to make a person feel important; simply saying a few kind words to a person especially if they seem low for some reason can make you win a friend in just a matter of minutes. Giving an acquaintance a genuine compliment or pointing out something you admire in them can easily win them over as a friend

4. Use names - A person who does not remember your name mainly because you think that the person is disinterested in you normally puts you off. The opposite of this then is also true. When you call a person by their name and keep referring them to their name, you make them feel important and this automatically makes them interested in knowing more about. If you are not good at remembering names, you come up with a clever way of mastering people's names.

How to Win People with Your Way of Thinking?

Tuning your mind to operate and think in a certain way when interacting with people can make help you develop a subconscious way of winning people over.

1. Being friendly

    Being friendly to every person you encounter, including complete strangers, can help you develop positive energy in you that attracts people. This should also be your first approach even when you encounter difficult people or find yourself in a predicament. Choosing to be friendly can warm people up and change the course of a difficult situation. Acting friendly all the time also prevents other people from labeling you as fake, especially when you do it to get something from them.

2. Let the other person do most of the talking

    This is a proven fact; people love the sound of their own voice. Therefore, whenever you encounter a new group of people you should let them do the majority of the talking. You might be surprised when you are referred to as the conversationalist when all you did was listen to a person go on and on about their interests. When you also allow people to express themselves without any interruptions, they feel good about themselves, which also makes them appreciate you even more.

3. Show respect to others' opinions

    No matter how much you disagree with a person's opinion, you should let them express it freely. You should never disregard another person's opinion just because you have different thoughts about the subject matter. The statement everyone is entitled to his or her own opinion applies here. A good way of trying to understand a person's opinion is to view things from their perspective and not yours.

4. Do not criticize or condemn or tell a person that they are wrong

    Again, people are entitled to think differently, so do not play judge and try to criticize or condemn people for their way of thinking. Silence is golden, especially during first encounters. The above actions are also likely to lead to intense arguments, which an individual should avoid lest people say regrettable things that they cannot take back. Winning an argument will also make you lose a potential friend while losing the same argument can humiliate you and bolster arrogance from the other party, neither of which is a good foundation for a healthy relationship.

5. Admit your mistakes

    Whenever you make a mistake, it is good to admit you are

wrong and apologize for it. Be empathetic about your mistake and quickly move on from it. By pointing out your wrongdoing, you make people develop a forgiving attitude, which is very healthy when trying to build relationships with people. When you also admit your mistakes, you appear trustworthy which is great.

6. Ask questions that require yes responses

If you want to win people easily, you must create a positive environment for people to communicate and exchange thoughts. As you begin to converse with a person, lean towards positive topics and avoid controversial ones such as politics. Asking questions that have yes responses that you both agree with keeps things positive and make it easier for the other person to continue agreeing more and more with you.

7. Letting people believe that they have good ideas

Although this may be hard for some people to do, it can certainly help in winning people. When you let people take credit for brilliant ideas that you have lured then into, you create an opportunity to win them over. Making it look like they have arrived at the idea from their own thinking gives you extra points as a potential friend.

How to Use Positive Influence and Not Manipulation to Win Friends

Manipulation involves controlling people in unscrupulous ways. Positive influence entails using acceptable tactics to win over friends. If a person is truly interested in establishing long-term meaningful relationships, then they will strive to use positive influence rather than manipulation to win people over. Some of the ways a person can do this are through the following:

1. Being authentic

   In order to influence people positively, you must be authentic. You should never try to be someone that you are

not this likely to backfire on you in the not so long future and jeopardize your young relationship. You should find whatever is unique to you and sell it like hotcakes.

2. Using expertise

People listen to titles and authority figures so if you have expertise in a certain area, you can use it to positively influence people and thus acquire friends. If you do not have any title or authority status, you can come up with a strategy to climb up the status ladder and be recognizable as an authority figure. Authority figures get leadership appointments and can take advantage of their position to influence people.

3. Leading by example

Another positive way of persuading people to a cause is to lead by example. People who inspire people by carrying out the very same act that they expect others to undertake are naturally able to sway people. Such people easily attract people who want to emulate them or be associated with them.

4. Looking for good

Constantly pointing out people's wrongs can make people lose interest in being associated with you. A person looking to win friends should do the opposite and focus on the good that people do instead of what is sometimes beyond their control and can, therefore, not achieve. People will hold you high and want to make friends with you because of your positivity and encouragement.

5. Praising and appreciating

In addition to focusing on mostly the good aspects of a person's personality, you can consider peppering people with genuine praise about their skills and attributes. Celebrating people's accomplishment inspires them to do better and seek for more acknowledgment and encouragement from you.

6. Not wanting to be right all the time

If you are ever to succeed in making and keeping new friends, you must give up the need to be right all the time. Rather than fighting over who is right, friends should strive to be kind to one another. Being right can sometimes hurt people's feeling and make a person look like a know it all which is an unattractive trait in a person who you would want to be your friend. Being right all the time can also make you appear as a bully, which again cannot win people over.

Chapter 7: Becoming a Good Conversationalist to Influence Other's Behavior

Conversation skills are fast becoming a lost art in the modern digital age. However, they are as important today as ever. People who engage in face-to-face conversations with ease tend to appear approachable and personable and often end up making lasting connections with others. This connection can subsequently help improve their careers and/or personal relationships.

Every good friendship, beautiful romance, or big business deal begins with a conversation. Great conversationalists are a joy to speak with because they seem to possess undeniable energy, sensitivity, and self-awareness. It is easy to hit it off immediately with such people because they seem to have endless things to talk about.

On the other hand, having a conversation with people who lack any conversational skills can be quite awkward and painful. Such people often answer questions with monosyllabic responses, and the conversation often turns into a monologue or trails off into long pauses. According to Frank Crane, the secrets to being a good conversationalist are a real unselfish interest in others and practice.

Many people have a hard time engaging in a conversation with people they do not know, or even with acquaintances. Whether one hates or loves networking, there is no denying the importance of engaging in face-to-face interactions. Whether one is engaging in a serious negotiation or engaging in small talk, how one communicates with other people will determine the outcome of that conversation.

Becoming a good conversationalist to influence others' behavior requires having the right set of skills in one's communication toolbox. Some people can talk about anything to anyone, while others have a difficult time making small talk. The difference between the two is not about finding something to talk about; rather, it is about polishing one's communication skills to keep a conversation flowing.

Some of the essential qualities of a good conversationalist are:

1. Active listening

2. Courtesy

3. Ability to know what and when to share

4. Knowing when to be silent

5. Being interesting, interested, and curious

6. Ability to leave the other person feeling good for having engaged in the conversation

Good conversations require a fair amount of give-and-take. When one person asks a question, for example, the other person should respond with an answer that will encourage the flow of conversation. It is like playing a game of catch. When one player throws the ball to another player, the one with the ball should pass the ball back without letting it drop.

How to Be a Good Conversationalist

Being a good conversationalist can open many doors. It is during face-to-face conversations that most people form instant opinions about whether they like, trust, and/or believe the person they are having a conversation with, even if it is a short conversation. Deep down, humans desperately want to be a part of a captivating conversation that allows them to learn, laugh, and remember the moment with longing.

Most of the best talk show hosts that people love are, at their core, great conversationalists. The best among them are witty conversationalists, great listeners and quick on their feet, which is why millions of people still watch those late-night talk shows with interest and joy. Some of the ways to cultivate good conversational skills include:

1. **Have a good mindset going in**

    It can be nerve-racking going into a new situation where one will need to interact with other people. However, going in with curiosity and the desire to learn more about other people will help improve one's interactions.

2. Be genuinely interested in the other person

People should be interested in the other person or people they are having a conversation with and ask themselves several important questions that will help them think of things to talk about and say. Some of the questions they should ask themselves include:

a. What is on this person's mind

b. Who is this person?

c. What motivates him/her?

d. What does he/she like doing?

To have a great conversation, it is important for their interest to be genuine, not artificial. When a conversation lacks a driving force behind it, it will likely fall flat. Actually, there is no reason to have a conversation with someone if one is not interested in him/her. It is better to move on to a person one really wants to talk to and know.

3. Focus on the positive

Focusing on positive topics will help conversations to flow more smoothly. For example, instead of talking about problems or past grievances, it is more helpful to a conversation to discuss future goals and positive experiences. If one feels the other party is comfortable with a particular negative topic, then it is okay to talk about it; however, the conversation should have a specific purpose.

It is also important to adopt a forward-thinking mentality during a conversation. This means more solutions and less complaining, or more empathy and less judgment. Having this type of mentality will make one a more interesting and enjoyable person to interact with; however, failure to adopt this mentality will transform one into an energy vampire.

4. Have a conversation, not an argument or debate

When a conversation turns argumentative, it quickly burns down into nothing. Having a demeaning and combative attitude when engaging in a conversation tends to be mentally and emotionally draining to the other person.

Good conversations are avenues through which people share their opinions, not a podium to air one's stance against another person's opinions. One can discuss ideas, but it is important to do so amiably. There is no need to come to an agreement or conclusion in every discussion. If two people cannot achieve convergence, they should leave things open.

5. Be respectful

Instead of judging, imposing, or criticizing, one should respect other people's views and opinions. It is fine to express one's view; however, one should avoid forcing it on other people. In addition, one should avoid encroaching on other people's space; instead, one should respect their personal choices without judgment.

6. Put others in their best light

During a conversation, one should look for ways to make the other person feel and look good. It is always a good idea to give credit where it is due and praise where appropriate. Many people do not recognize or believe in their personal abilities; allowing them to shine in their own light is a sign of good conversational skills.

7. Build on commonalities while embracing differences

Although people are different, they still have many commonalities between them. Differences make people unique, so it is important to embrace them. When there are clashes in different ideas, people should simply agree to disagree. While conversing with another person, one should look for any commonalities to establish a link and build on that. In fact, this is a great way to learn more about another person, which will help improve the quality of the conversation.

8. Be true to self

Every individual's best asset is his/her true self; therefore, it is important to embrace it and let it shine through, instead of covering it up. A conversation where one person is simply miming the other party's words tends to be painfully boring and unfulfilling because there will be nothing new or interesting to talk about.

People who are true to themselves are usually more comfortable sharing their real opinions and thoughts in a respectful and effective manner. In addition, they are proud of who they are and what they stand for and are happy to expose their real selves to others, making them good conversationalists and influences.

9. Equal sharing

Great conversations often consist of fair sharing by both parties. Depending on the situation and circumstances, this sharing maybe 50-50, 60-40, or 40-60, but the idea is that both parties should have a fair opportunity to contribute to the conversation.

Having the gift of gab does not necessarily mean that one is a good conversationalist. A good conversationalist should be sensitive enough to actively listen to the other person and pose relevant questions that prove that one is focusing on the conversation. It also means taking the initiative to share more about oneself if the other party has done the same.

In addition, the other person does not need to ask

questions for one to share. Some people simply do not think it is polite to ask questions while having a conversation because they believe it may be invasive and rude.

10. **Give and take**

During a conversation, some people have a tendency to say some shockingly weird stuff, such as a dirty joke or distasteful remark, which can make the other party react in a negative way. Good conversationalists, however, are often in control of their emotions. They will give the person the benefit of the doubt instead of judging him/her straight away. At one time or another, everyone makes some oddball comments. It is better to simply shrug it off or laugh and consider it funny conversation banter.

Starting A Conversation

As a social construct, a conversation serves as a building block for the establishment and maintenance of different types of relationships. If navigated properly and successfully, it can serve as a gateway to lead people to the information and/or outcome they desire. On the surface, conversations can look like simple exchanges of ideas and thoughts. However, in reality, they offer massive opportunities to uncover new information; build and strengthen relationships; and share ideas, thoughts, or information one possesses.

Often, people do not have a lot of room to maneuver in terms of conversational patterns and topics when talking to work colleagues or strangers. It is easier to tell a close friend about an exciting event or an idea than it is to tell a total stranger. However, people with excellent conversational skills can steer any interaction, even a seemingly innocuous one, in any direction they need it to go. Knowing how to start a conversation is the first step towards gaining these skills.

Some of the best ways to start a conversation with the ability to head in the desired direction include:

a) Start with a compliment to instantly flatter the recipient and make him/her warm-up and be more willing to participate in the conversation

b) Start with sports or the weather to open other avenues for further exploration

c) Talk about the venue

d) Ask a simple favor to spark an inherent connection with the other party

e) Tell a clean, intelligent joke to make the other person smile, which will create a sympathetic connection that might hold for the entire conversation

f) Start with any observation, however innocuous it may be,

and then guide the resulting conversation in the desired direction

g) Ask a targeted question related to one's intended topic of conversation

Having made the first step to start a conversation that might lead just about anywhere, one will have the opportunity to use a series of directional questions and responses to lead the conversation to one's intended topic.

About Active Listening

Active listening is one of the most critical aspects of becoming a good conversationalist to influence others' behavior. However, it is difficult to master this skill. Fortunately, with adequate practice, time, and patience, anyone can cultivate and develop this skill. As the name suggests, active listening is the process of fully focusing on what someone else is saying and understanding his/her meaning, instead of simply hearing his/her message.

It involves taking note of non-verbal communication and listening with all senses, in addition to giving full attention to the person speaking. Otherwise, the speaker might think that what he/she is saying is uninteresting or boring to the listener. A good conversationalist will convey active listening by using both non-verbal and verbal messages, such as encouraging the speaker to continue, maintaining eye contact, nodding his/her head, and using other forms of non-verbal cues.

Active listening is one of the most important aspects of interpersonal communication. Listening is not just hearing; rather, it is an active and intentional process by which one person decides to listen to what someone else is saying, with the full intention of understanding his/her message.

Some of the common signs of listening include asking relevant questions, smiling, avoiding distractions, reflecting the speaker's facial expressions, using the right posture, maintaining eye contact, using positive reinforcement, clarifying certain matters, paraphrasing, remembering important points, and summarizing what the other person just said.

Good conversational skills have the ability to influence other people's behavior. It is normal for people to come across situations where they need to influence others in social settings, professional settings, or even personal settings. This influence may be in the form of inspiring others, creating relationships, gaining support, persuading other people, or engaging people's imagination. Whatever form it takes, being a good conversationalist makes a person's job easier.

Chapter 8: Read Other People's Body Language

About Non-Verbal Communication

Non-verbal communication is the process of exchanging information using body language, personal appearance, touch, gestures, postures, and proxemics. It is passing on a message by use of any other medium other than writing or speech. Non-verbal communication can make or break the message you are trying to portray. When you use the correct body signals and gestures, the message conveyed is usually positive. When your body signals do not match your verbal message, then it is possible to convey the wrong message.

Non-verbal communication plays a big role in telling if one is being truthful and the success at which he or she is paying attention. If your body signals match your verbal message, they increase trust, clarity, and rapport and when they do not, they can build tension, confusion, and mistrust.

Non-verbal communication has a strong effect on first impressions. This is because the way a person portrays himself or herself on the first encounter is non-verbal communication to the observer. It actually just takes the first four seconds of meeting someone to form an impression. Non-verbal communication has more meaning than verbal communication.

Non-verbal communication plays the following roles:

1. Repetition- Non-verbal communication repeats and can strengthen your verbal message. For example, when we say yes while nodding our heads

2. Contradiction- Non-verbal communication can also contradict the message conveyed, for example when someone says they had fun while using a flat voice and does not show emotions, the two messages contradict

3. Complementing- Non-verbal communication can complement the message conveyed. For example, if you applaud someone for winning a race in addition to giving them a gift, it increases the message's impact.

4. Accenting- Non-verbal communication can emphasize the message a sender is trying to convey. For example, you can use gestures, change your pitch, volume or deliberately pause to accent the message.

5. Substitution- Sometimes non-verbal communication can substitute the verbal message. For example, people will understand the description of a short person more when shown using hand signals than when they get their actual height figures.

Non-verbal communication typically involves the process of

encoding and decoding messages. Encoding involves coming up with information using gestures, postures, touch, body movements and facial expressions while decoding is the process of interpreting the information received from the encoder. Encoding requires the use of signals known universally and decoding requires the use of knowledge one may have of certain things. For example, when an encoder who is traffic police raises his hand at a roundabout, the decoder may know from experiences that the officer is signaling him or her to stop.

Non-verbal communication focuses on three principal areas:

- The environment where communication takes place

- The physical characteristics of the encoder

- How the communicators behave while conversing

Studies have shown that non-verbal communication represents two-thirds of all communication therefore if you want to improve your communication skills, it is important to be keen on not only other people's non-verbal communication but also your own.

Types of Non-Verbal Communication

There are various types of non-verbal communication:

1. Kinesics or Body Language

This type of non-verbal communication has a relationship with body movement. It is how we communicate non-verbally using our bodies.

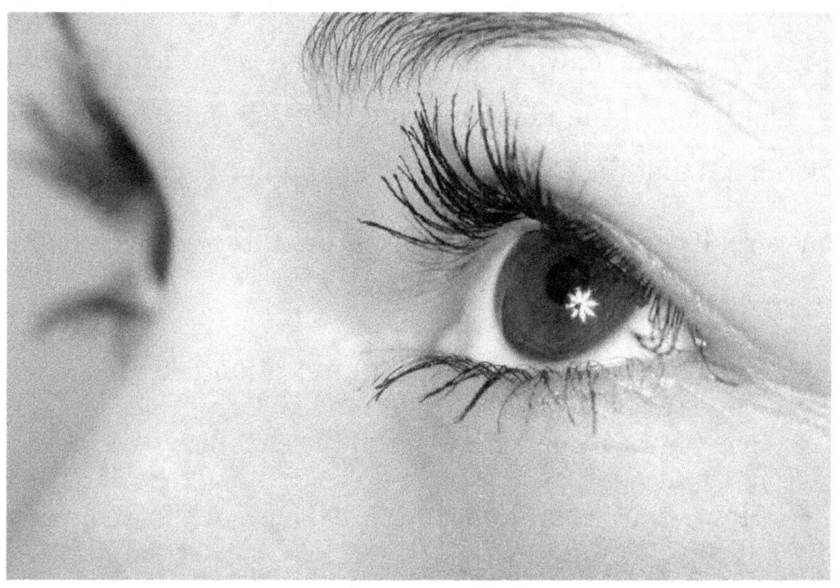

1. Face - The face and eyes actually show non-verbal communication. You can node, shake your head, smile, wink, laugh, yawn using different parts of your face.

2. Eye Contact - The eyes also portray important cues. You can indicate interest, attention, engagement, and involvement by how you look, stare, blink wink, move your eyebrows or maintain eye contact. Our

pupils dilate more when an individual is interested. Maintaining eye contact and the duration of eye contact is associated with telling the truth while shifting your eyes is associated with lying or lack of interest.

3. Posture - Body postures speak a lot about someone's character, attitude, and feelings. Non-verbal cues like slouching, sitting upright, arms crossing, legs spreading and leg-crossing can communicate a variety of messages whether good or bad. One can be able to tell if someone is paying attention, likes you, and dislikes you by looking at his or her postures. Situations influence posture. People use different postures in different setups. For example, one is likely to sit upright in an interview and slouch a bit when on a social gathering.

4. Gestures - This cue involves the use of body motions to express the message someone is conveying. Sometimes we use gestures like waving, pointing, doing a thumbs up even without thinking because we were probably brought up around people who used them. Some gestures, however, vary across cultures. For example, snapping fingers may be asking someone to hurry up in some cultures while in other cultures when you snap your figures close

to someone's face it is offensive. It is important to use gestures according to how an individual is interpreting them in a specific culture to avoid misinterpretation.

2. Paralanguage or Vocalics

This non-verbal communication focuses on speech signals such as pitch, volume, rate of speech and intonation. With this type of communication, there is the production of noise. A good example of the use of paralanguage is someone saying that he or she is happy with a blank facial expression and a toned-down voice. The facial expression here contradicts the verbal message.

Other specific forms of paralinguistic respiration include gasps which convey a message of panic or difficult breathing, sighs which mostly convey a negative emotion, throat-clearing coveys the arrival of someone's presence in a room and lastly hmm noises which indicate one wants to pause and think.

3. Haptics or touch

This type of non-verbal communication uses the sense of touch. It refers to how we communicate through touch. How we use our sense of touch communicates a particular message; for example, handshakes, holding hands, slapping someone on the back or high fives are all ways we use our sense of touch to communicate. You can also convey certain feelings when you touch yourself in certain manners like scratching or pounding on your chest.

People use touch to communicate sympathy, affection, and familiarity. The meaning of touch depends on the situation, someone's culture, the manner of touch and the relationship between the communicators.

4. Chronemics

This non-verbal communication is the role of time in communication. It involves how human beings use time, value time, structure their time and reacts to period communication. Examples of time perceptions include one's ability or inability to wait, and punctuality.

Different cultures perceive time differently, which in turn influences communication. For example, some cultures consider a monochromic time system where people do things one at a time or a polychromic time system where people do several things at once.

5. Personal Appearance

How we dress, our choice of color, hairstyles, and jewelry are non-verbal communication. Human beings tend to judge others based on their appearances. For example, when you dress in bright clothing, it brings out a happy mood and when you dress dull, it brings out a sad mood.

According to various studies how we look and present

ourselves plays a role in how people perceive us and even how much they earn. The choices we make about our personal appearance most of the time have meaning to those around us. They dictate the image one wishes to put forth.

6. Proxemics

This non-verbal cue deals with the amount of space one feels is necessary to set between them and others. Age, gender, and culture influence proxemics. Proxemics has four   main   sections:

1. Intimate space - This is any distance less than 18 inches. Usually used by people who feel comfortable around each other like a spouse or child

2. Personal space - This is between 18 inches and 4 feet used by people when interacting as friends

3. Social space – This is between 4 ft. and 12 feet. It is the most used space and is often used when communicating with classmates or colleagues

4. Public space – This is anything greater than 12 feet. It is the longest gap often between an individual and an   audience

The above sections vary greatly depending on the relationship you have with the person, feelings, intimacy, and comfort.

Maintain Positive Body Language

Body language is a form of non-verbal communication where you use body language and gestures to convey a message. Positive body language occurs when someone receives the message positively or with enthusiasm. Positive body language usually adds strength to our verbal messages.

Here are tips on how to maintain positive body language:

1. Eye contact - It is important to maintain eye contact with the person you are conversing with. Keep your eyes locked a few seconds at a time and remember to blink and avoid staring. Positive eye contact portrays that you are interested in the conversation.

2. Posture - Maintain an open posture. Always keep a relaxed posture, avoid slouching or keeping your back too stiff. When you are relaxed, it shows that you are comfortable.

3. Arms and Hands - Always keep your hands at the sides and avoid crossing them. This sends the message that you are open to what the other person is saying. You can only use your hands to gesture when you speak; this emphasizes and compliments your message even more. Lastly, always

greet people using a firm handshake; take care not to be too firm. It actually sets the tone for the conversation. It is also important to learn about various cultures' greetings beforehand.

4. Leaning - always maintain a forward lean as opposed to a back one. When you lean forward when someone is talking, it shows you are paying attention and actively listening

5. Feet Movement - When you watch someone's feet, you are able to see how he or she feel. To maintain positivity, if seated, keep your legs apart a bit and avoid fidgeting or shuffling; it shows confidence.

6. Affirmative actions - You can also maintain positive body language by nodding your head, doing a thumbs-up or smiling. This shows people that you can identify with what they are saying, agree with them and are listening to them.

7. Mirroring - This involves mimicking the gestures, postures, and speech patterns of the other person in a good way while avoiding mockery. It makes the other person feel more connected to the person doing the mirroring. When you share similar gestures and attitudes, the other person will be more willing to empathize with you.

8. Voice - Always ensure to keep your voice audible. Do not speak too fast or too slow. Take in between pauses to breath and ensure your tone and pitch is right. The pauses

will help you calm down if you are nervous.

9. If you are in a business forum, take notes. This shows that your level of engagement and respect for the person speaking. Raise your head up regularly to maintain eye contact.

Avoid Negative Body Language

Negative body language occurs when we either consciously or unconsciously use non-verbal communication to express negative feelings. For example, anger, boredom, impatience, or lack of confidence. Here is how to avoid negative body language:

1. Avoiding Eye Contact - when you talk to another person while looking at the floor or just around him or her, it shows you are not confident in yourself or the message you are trying to convey. When conversing always maintain natural eye contact and avoid blinking too much. Rapid blinking communicates that you are feeling uncomfortable with the conversation.

2. Forced Smile - It is very easy to spot a forced or fake smile. So, avoid fake smiling at others.

3. Crossing Your Arms - Crossing your arms or even pocketing is mostly a negative body language especially when someone is talking to you. It comes out as defensive,

arrogant, and impatient. To avoid this, always keep your hand at the sides and only bring them up when making a gesture.

4. Covering Your Sensitive Parts - Most people do this subconsciously; they will keep covering up the places on their bodies they are vulnerable about like their genitals or stomach. This shows a lack of confidence and nervousness. To avoid this, always wear something you feel confident in and be proud of how you look.

5. Fidgeting with Objects - When conversing with someone there is no quick way of letting him or her know that you are not paying attention or are impatient than when you fidget with objects near you. To avoid this, put away any objects that you may start fiddling with when conversing.

6. Feet - People who lack confidence or are nervous will shuffle, fidget with their feet, or slightly kick their feet. Usually, most people do this subconsciously. To avoid this, remember to keep your feet open and relaxed and avoid fidgeting.

7. Poor Posture - When you slouch your back and shoulders and cave in your chest when you sit or stand, it shows that you lack confidence and it is a sign of surrender. Always ensure you maintain an upright position but do not be too stiff either, make it as natural as possible.

8. Handshakes - Sometimes we can get carried away with the

handshakes and they become awkward or, worse, we end up squeezing other people's hands so tight, it becomes painful. This comes out as rude and aggressive. To avoid this, use a firm handshake but do not squeeze too tight.

9. Leaning - When we lean away from the person speaking, it shows you are disinterested or impatient. Always lean forward to show that you are interested in and are paying attention.

10. Touching Your facial Features - Most of the time when you touch your face while talking to someone, you portray a negative image. You may look disinterested, nervous, or distracted. Avoid touching your face. Touching your nose is a known cue for lying.

11. Unproductive use of space - When speaking to a large audience you might be tempted to stand on one position like a statute. This again shows a lack of confidence. To avoid this, learn how to use all the stage space given, this tells the audience you are confident and comfortable being there. Engaging your audience can also help you use the space well.

12. Biting Your Lip - Most of the time, people bit their lips subconsciously. They do it when they are unsure, have made a mistake or are not confident about what they are saying. You tend to lose the attention of those around you by doing so. Avoid biting your lips.

How to Read Body Language?

The body language of the people around us speaks volumes; it reveals what someone is thinking. In fact, people communicate more using their body language than by speaking verbally. Therefore, the art of learning to read body language is very important. Here are some of the ways we can read people's body language:

1. Study the eyes

    When you look at someone's eyes when talking to him or her, you can learn a lot about how they feel on the inside. If the person avoids making eye contact, it can indicate that they are shy or bored. If a person looks away to the side, they show deceit and if a person looks down, it shows nervousness or submissiveness.

2. Another thing you can note is whether their pupils are dilated or not. This can be hard to detect however if you notice someone has dilated pupils it means they are responding positively towards you. A person's blinking rate can also speak volumes. When they blink too much it may indicate someone is lying, however, when they do not blink, someone is outright staring at you. When they glance at something, it may show their desire for something. For example, when they glance at the clock, it means they are bored and want to leave.

3. Look at Facial Expressions

People have mastered how to control their facial expressions however; you can still notice a few things by observing their expressions. A frown indicates disapproval or unhappiness. Watch for smiles as it shows the person agrees and is interested in what you are saying. Be keep to note whether it is a genuine smile or not. People usually express a genuine smile using the whole face while a fake one only uses the mouth. Fake smiles hide dissatisfaction.

4. Observe closely for mirroring cues

They say imitation is the best form of flattery. When you

notice the other person mimicking your body language, they are genuinely giving you a compliment and trying to establish a rapport with you. If you lean on a desk, wait to see if the other person leans as well.

5. Check on proximity

    This is the distance maintained between you and the other person. If the person is standing close to you, they may view you favorably, if they back up or move away when you move closer, they may not be interested. However, it is important to avoid invading too much on people's personal space; they may start to feel uncomfortable.

6. Pay attention to feet movement

    People tend to concentrate on their hand gestures and facial expressions and forget about their feet. Feet reveal a lot about someone. When sitting down people point their feet towards the direction they want to go, so if it is towards you, then they hold you favorably. When they point feet towards the side, they are not interested and would like to talk to the other person. If they shuffle or fidget, they might be nervous.

7. Hand signals

    Hands also have a way of revealing information about a person. Pocketing or touching the face indicates deception or nervousness. Supporting your head with one hand resting on a table may indicate attentiveness or he or she is trying to focus while supporting with two hands shows boredom.

8. Arm position

    Observe if the person had crossed arms or open arms. Crossed arms indicate defensiveness, impatience, and someone is probably closed-minded. However, if accompanied by other expressions like a smile it may indicate confidence and a relaxed attitude. Placing your hand on the hips shows dominance.

9. The mouth

    Observing the mouth is also essential in reading body language. When someone covers their mouth, they may be trying to be polite when coughing, yawning, or sneezing. When they bit their lower lip, it may indicate fear or worry. When they tighten their lips, they may indicate disapproval or distrust. When they turn their mouth slightly up, they might be holding you favorable but when they turn it slightly down, they disapprove or feel sad.

10. Gestures

    Gestures give out obvious body signals. We can use our fingers to show numerical amounts. Waving and pointing indicate common gestures. However, gestures might be hard to read across cultures especially if they have different interpretations. For example, the V-sign may indicate victory or peace in some countries while in others it might have an offensive meaning. Therefore, how we interpret gestures may vary across cultures.

11. Posture

We can tell a lot by observing someone's posture. An open posture indicated openness and friendliness while a closed posture indicates hostility and unfriendliness. Postures let us know how someone feels and shows a hint of their personality.

Chapter 9: Develop Emotional Awareness

When it comes to achieving success in one's personal life and career, emotional awareness may be more important than IQ. Emotional awareness is the measure of a person's ability to recognize and control his/her emotions, as well as other people's emotions.

Developing this ability also helps people to notice and understand what others are feeling. For the most part, this recognition and understanding of emotions is a non-verbal process that informs people's thinking and determines how well they interact and connect with others.

People who consciously choose to develop their emotional awareness are better able to connect with their feelings, make smarter decisions about important matters, and turn intention into action. This awareness has an effect on different aspects of an individual's life, including:

1. Performance at work or school

2. Mental health

3. Physical health

4. Relationships

5. Social intelligence

When it comes to developing this ability, people need to understand that there is a difference between simply learning about it and applying that critical knowledge in their lives. In other words, just because a person knows that he/she should do something does not mean that he/she will do it, especially if he/she is experiencing a lot of stress.

Therefore, it is important to learn how to manage and overcome stress to remain emotionally aware. Some of the abilities and skills that come with developing emotional awareness include:

a) Self-emotion

b) Ability to adapt to change

c) Self-control

d) Self-confidence

e) Conflict resolution skills

f) Negotiation skills

g) Empathy

Steps to Develop Emotional Awareness

Some people seem to have a naturally high level of emotional awareness. No matter what kind of problem they are facing or the situation they are in, they always seem to be in control. They always seem to know the right thing to say things and the right behavior or reaction. In fact, it is almost impossible to see them upset, angry, or offended.

In most cases, however, such people took the time and made the effort to cultivate and develop their emotional awareness. By developing this skill, one's brain will adapt to make such reactions and behaviors automatic, and slowly get rid of the negative responses and behaviors. Developing emotional awareness involves the cultivation of several of its fundamental features, including:

Social Awareness

With practice, patience, and time, people can learn to develop these critical features of emotional awareness. Human beings have different needs and wants, and different ways of expressing their emotions. Navigating through these emotions takes cleverness and tact, which is where emotional awareness comes into play.

Having social skills, or social awareness enables people to identify and interpret the verbal and non-verbal messages other people constantly send in the process of communication. These messages help people read and understand how others are feeling, what is most important to them, and how their emotions are changing from time to time. Essentially, mindfulness is an important ally or social awareness.

To develop social awareness, one needs to understand the importance of being mindful towards others. It is impossible to notice non-verbal messages when one is thinking about other things or lost in one's head. Developing this ability requires one's presence of mind, which means doing the following things:

a) Focusing on interaction and setting other thoughts aside

b) Paying attention to others to gain insight into their emotional state, which will also reveal one's emotional state as well

c) Paying attention to one's own emotional flow

Self-awareness

Another way to develop emotional awareness is by being self-aware. The ability to connect with one's emotions is the secret to understanding how they influence one's actions and thoughts. Some of the questions to consider when it comes to self-awareness include:

a) Do you experience one emotion after another as situations change from one moment to another?

b) Do you experience strong feelings that capture your attention and that of others?

c) Do physical sensations accompany your emotions?

d) Do you pay attention to your feelings and their consequences?

e) Do you experience individual emotions and feelings, each of which manifests in subtle facial expressions?

If any of these experiences sound strange or is unfamiliar, one likely lacks the appropriate level of self-awareness. To develop this ability and achieve emotional health, one needs to reconnect with one's core emotions, understand them, embrace them, and be comfortable with them. This is only possible through the practice of mindfulness.

This is the act of intentionally focusing on the present moment without any judgment. Mindfulness will help shift one's attention on, or preoccupation with, thoughts towards an understanding and appreciation of the moment, including one's emotional and physical sensations. Consequently, one will gain a larger perspective on the situation and on life itself. In addition, mindfulness focuses and calms people, making them more self-aware and emotionally aware of the process.

Motivation

People who are motivated usually have a high level of emotional awareness, which also gives them the ability and willingness to postpone immediate results for more important long-term success. In addition, they love a challenge, are highly productive, and tend to be very effective in everything they do.

Empathy

This is another important element of emotional awareness. It is the ability to identify and understand the views, needs, and wants of others. People with this quality are very good at recognizing and understanding other people's feelings and emotions, even when they may not be so obvious.

Consequently, they are excellent at actively listening to others, building relationships, and managing those relationships. In addition, they do not judge others prematurely or stereotype. Essentially, they tend to live their lives in an honest and open manner.

Self-Management

In order for people to engage their emotional awareness, they need to control their emotions to use them to make positive decisions about their actions and behavior. When most people experience extreme stress, they often lose control of their emotions, which negatively affects their ability to act appropriately and thoughtfully.

Obviously, it is not easy to make a rational decision when one's stress levels are overwhelming. Extreme stress can compromise one's ability to think clearly and accurately analyze one's emotions and other people's emotions. That said emotions act as important pieces of information to inform people about themselves and others.

However, in the midst of a stressful situation that takes people out of their comfort zone, they tend to lose control of themselves. Fortunately, when people develop their ability to stay emotionally present and manage stress, they learn to handle upsetting or stressful situations without letting them override their self-control and thoughts.

In addition, they are better able to make smarter choices that allow them to take initiative, control impulse behaviors and feelings, follow through on commitments, manage their emotions in a healthy manner, and adapt to shifting circumstances.

Relationship Management

The ability to collaborate with other people is a critical process that starts with one's ability to recognize and understand what others are feeling or experiencing, which is an important aspect of emotional awareness. In addition, once a person develops emotional awareness, he/she can effectively develop other important life skills that will help make his/her relationships more fulfilling, fruitful, and effective.

People need to be aware of how effectively they employ non-verbal cues. For a fact, it is impossible to communicate without sending non-verbal messages to other people about how one is feeling. The muscles in people's faces, especially those in the forehead, mouth, nose, and around the eyes, communicate in a non-verbal manner how they are feeling.

Even when people try to ignore or hide their feelings, the emotional part of their brain, which is always alert, will convey their emotions using certain facial and body movements or expressions. The ability to identify and understand the non-verbal cues that one sends to other people plays an important part in improving one's relationship.

Another important aspect of relationship management is humor. Play, laughter, and humor are natural and effective antidotes to anger and stress. Humor helps people get rid of some of their emotional baggage, in addition to helping them keep things in perspective. Having a good laugh can also help relieve stress, restore balance to one's nervous system, sharpen one's mind, calm one down, and make one more empathetic.

Learning to consider conflict as a great opportunity to learn about others and grow closer to them is another way to develop one's relationship management skills. In human relationships, disagreements and conflicts are inevitable. It is impossible for everyone to have the same expectations, views, and needs at all times, which is actually a good thing. Life would be boring if everyone was the same.

However, to improve relationship management skills as a way to develop emotional awareness, people need to resolve conflict in a constructive and healthy way, which will strengthen trust between them. In fact, people do not need to perceive conflict as punishing or threatening; instead, they need to understand that it can help foster safety, creativity, and freedom in relationships.

Self-Confidence

Self-confidence is one of the most important facets of emotional awareness. Essentially, it is the emotional component of one's personality and is usually present in people who have their act together and display a positive attitude towards themselves and others without being arrogant.

Self-confidence consists of a fundamental belief that one can do whatever is necessary to achieve the desired outcome. When any sort of obstacle or problem arises, people with self-confidence continue to believe in their abilities and work towards overcoming the barriers, instead of giving up. A person's level of self-confidence determines what he/she can make happen in any aspect of life.

A person lacking self-confidence will not persevere in the event he/she comes across some sort of difficulty or barrier; in fact, he/she might not even try. That said arrogance is another confidence problem that is equally incompatible with emotional awareness as a lack of self-confidence. In fact, pseudo-confidence or overconfidence can be quite destructive to a person's personal, social, and/or professional life.

As self-confidence is likely to result from positive social experiences and social confidence, it is an important aspect when it comes to developing emotional awareness, which plays an important part in fostering positive social experiences requisite to building self-esteem. Essentially, self-confidence influences emotional awareness, which in turn influences people's lives in a positive way.

Self-confidence can have a huge effect on almost all aspects of a person's life; unfortunately, so many people have a difficult time achieving it, which can lead to a vicious circle. Without self-confidence, one will probably lack self-awareness, which will make it more difficult to achieve success in different aspects and areas of life.

The good news is that anyone can learn to be more self-confident and build on it to achieve the desired goals. Whether an individual is working on his/her self-confidence or trying to build other people's confidence, it is well worth the effort. People's level of self-confidence shows in many different ways, such as through their body language, behavior, what they say, how they speak, and other ways.

Self-esteem and self-efficacy are the two main building blocks of self-confidence. People gain a sense of self-efficacy when they view themselves and others like them achieving goals and mastering skills that matter to them. This form of confidence comes with success, after learning and working hard to achieve that success. People with this type of confidence are better able to accept challenges and persevere in the face of setbacks.

Self-esteem, on the other hand, is a more general sense of confidence that one will be able to cope with whatever is happening in one's life. It is also a belief that one is right to be happy. In part, this type of confidence comes from the belief that other people approve of who one is; however, it also comes from the feeling that one is competent and/or is behaving in the right manner. Self-confidence is important to one's psychological well-being and health, in addition to being an important aspect of one's emotional awareness.

Although IQ can play a huge role when it comes to success in life, emotional awareness is critical to achieving one's goals and relating to others. These two abilities are at least equal to each other, which is why an increasing number of organizations are testing emotional intelligence when hiring new personnel. Regardless of their actual strengths and abilities, emotionally aware individuals tend to look at themselves more honestly, which allows them to handle criticism and use it to improve themselves and their performance.

Chapter 10: How to Become More Likeable

Most of us at some point in life have had a feeling of not being liked despite having supportive family and friends. We all wish that we could be liked and admired more by the people around us whether at work, school, or home.

However, we also need to ask ourselves about how we make other people feel when they are around us. Do they feel comfortable, appreciated, and accepted by us? Some people may think that likable people were born charming, but in reality, likeability skills can be learned. Likable people are often down-to-earth, warm, emotionally stable, trustworthy, and open. Listed below are some of the qualities that you need to have to be likable and the good thing is that these skills can be learned.

Trust and Honesty

The foundations of good relationships are built on trust and honesty. The more someone trusts you the more likely that person will share information, cooperate, and work with you effectively. If you want to be trusted, then you need to be honest and transparent.

You cannot create a trust if you keep on lying. Honesty is an important element in a relationship because it creates trust and helps us to live in reality and not fantasy. Even in an organization, trust between the staff and management increases the level of performance. Below are some key elements that can help us to build honesty and trust:

a) Understand yourself and what you want

For us to be honest with other people, we need to understand ourselves first. We need to know our perception of our surroundings and the people around us. Sometimes we do something not because we want to, but because everyone else is doing it or because of culture. It is good to differentiate what we want from what people want for us. This way we can be honest with ourselves and with the people around us.

b) Let your actions match your words

Do not preach water yet you drink wine! If you love

someone, do not just say it but also do things that will show him or her that you truly love him or her. Our behaviors should speak louder than words.

c) Be open to feedback

We should always be ready to listen to other people and try to see things from their point of view. We should allow others to tell us what they feel about us and we should not punish or react to feedback. This will enable others to be open to us and we shall have an honest relationship.

d) Accept the other person the way he/she is

No matter how connected we are to someone, we sometimes have different opinions on different things. If we do not see things from other people's point of view, it does not mean they are wrong or lying. It simply means they see things from a different perspective. If we are honest with one another, then we will be able to accept one another for who we truly are.

Patience

Can you tolerate waiting, delay, and frustration without getting upset? We have lost control of our patience at least a couple of times in our day-to-day activities. For example, you are going for a meeting and then you find yourself caught up in traffic for half an hour. You start sweating and feeling stressed up. Does this feeling sound familiar?

When we lose control of our patience, we not only hurt ourselves but even those people around us because we sometimes throw insults at them. Our stress levels also go up, we get headaches, and this is not good for our health.

Impatient people are always arrogant, insensitive, and short-tempered. These people always make quick decisions and judgments, which can be wrong. This attitude can affect a relationship at work or at home. People can learn patience just like any other skill.

Benefits of Developing Patience

- **Reduces stress levels**

  Impatience increases stress levels so when you learn to be patient, you are in control of your emotions and you do not get angry easily. This will help you handle difficult situations easily with some calmness.

- **Helps you make better decisions**

  When you are patient, you do not rush to making judgments and decisions, but you take time to analyze the situation at hand and come up with a solution. This will minimize making mistakes and errors.

- **Helps you to develop empathy and compassion**

  Patient people take time to understand what other people go through. This will help them to be compassionate towards others hence they create better relationships.

- **Helps you to understand and value the process of growth**

  Patience will help you start a project and give you that zeal to work on it to its completion. Patience will help that business of yours by giving it time to grow to its full potential. It does not demand results overnight, but it gives it time.

Tips to Help You Develop Patience

- **Recognize your impatience**

  Try to understand what makes you impatient; is it the urge to do things in a rush? Write down those things that stress you out and look for ways to dealing with them. If you are overwhelmed with work, just slow down and focus on one task at a time.

- **Look into the source of your impatience**

  Do you feel like time is not enough for you to do all the work? Then perhaps you should plan your time well. Try to schedule work that you can finish so that you are not overwhelmed.

- **Practice delayed gratification**

  When you want to go for that Pizza, stop and think first because maybe you do not need it after all. You can save that money and buy something else, which is more important.

- **Practice thinking before you speak**

  We need to be patient and weigh our words before speaking to avoid offending others.

Empathy

Empathy simply means putting yourself in someone else's shoes to understand what they feel or go through. It involves trying to be aware of other people's feelings and emotions. There are three types of empathy:

- Cognitive Empathy - putting yourself in someone else's place to see their point of view

- Emotional Empathy – feeling other people's emotion and catching the emotions e.g. crying with a bereaved person

- Compassionate Empathy – feeling other people's emotion and taking action to help

- Here are some proven ways that can help you to improve your empathy

- Challenge yourself - tackle challenging experiences, which can take you out of your comfort zone. Try to do something new that will humble you.

- Get out of your normal environment – travel to other places and experience different cultures.

- Develop some emotional intelligence – read books that talk about personal relationships and emotions.

- Get feedback – listen to the responses o of other people and check on them regularly to know how they are doing.

Active Listening

Active listening is a very important skill that we should all have. It refers to listening to someone attentively as they speak, rephrasing and reflecting on what they are saying while withholding judgment. You are supposed to give full attention to the speaker and then you give a response on what was said afterward.

Active listening is a skill that an individual can learn and develop with practice. This skill can have a positive impact on your job effectiveness and your relationships both at work and at home. This is because it makes someone feel as if the other person is hearing and valuing him or her.

Three Components to Active Listening

1. Comprehend: the listener should try to understand the speaker by paying attention to the speaker's verbal and non-verbal language.

2. Retain: the listener should memorize the important points of the speaker's message. They can write down the key points.

3. Respond: you give your response depending on how you

understood the speaker's message. You should do this after analyzing and remembering what the speaker said.

Features of Active Listening

- Eye contact: it is encouraging to look at the speaker as they speak. People can combine this with a smile and other non-verbal languages.

- Smile and nods

- Posture: signs of active listening can be leaning slightly forward or if the person is sitting, they can lean sideways. Another way is slanting the head or resting the head on the hand.

- Neutral and non-judgmental

- Avoid distractions

- Asking questions

- Reflecting on what was said

- Asking for clarification

- Positive feedback

How to Improve Your Active Listening Skills

a) Face the speaker - You should maintain eye contact with the person you are having the conversation with. Avoid looking at your phone, watch or other people. If you are not comfortable with looking into the eyes, you can look at other parts of their face or even the shoulder.

b) Picture the message - Try to form images on your mind about what is being communicated.

c) Withhold judgment - You should pay full attention and do not give your opinion before the speaker finishes talking.

d) Do not interrupt - You will not be able to grasp all the information when you interrupt the speaker and you will sound rude. Never try to finish the speaker's sentences even if you know what they are going to say next. You can ask questions or give your opinions later.

e) Reflect and clarify - This will ensure that you understood the speaker's message and you are reading from the same page. Reflecting means repeating what was said in your own words to make them know you understood the message. Clarifying means, you ask questions about what you did not understand.

f) Summarize - You explain the key points of the overall message of the speaker.

g) Respond - After listening carefully and analyzing the message, it is now your turn to give your opinion or ideas into the conversation. Remember you have to listen actively to have the privilege of sharing your thoughts.

Conflict Resolution

We all experience conflict at some point in our lives whether at home or at the workplace. Conflicts in the workplace if not handled properly can affect work productivity. Conflict resolution is the process of trying to resolve a dispute. There are different styles of conflict management. Here are some of the core skills used in conflict resolution.

Five Strategies of Conflict Resolution

1. Avoiding

   This is where both parties pretend that there is no problem. They just ignore and withdraw from the conflict. This is a common approach and it often works. It is used in those conflicts, which are not serious and are bound to resolve itself with time.

2. Competing

   This is a win or lose situation whereby the person with greater strength wins the conflict. This is not a good strategy for solving a problem since it does not give room for the losing side to express their concerns.

3. Accommodating

Being accommodating is a situation whereby one party gives in to the demands of another for the sake of maintaining harmony. Both parties prefer preserving the relationship than resolving the conflict. This can result in unresolved issues.

4. Collaborating

This method involves both parties coming together to find a solution to their conflict. This method requires an input of time for both parties to come up with a solution that is agreeable to all.

5. Compromising

Compromise is a situation where both parties give up on something to come up to an agreed mid-point. No one individual gets complete satisfaction from the results but it is a fair method.

Interest

Interest refers to having a strong urge to give attention to something or someone. When you want to create a good relationship with someone, look for those interests that you share. These could be shared hobbies. If you are meeting someone new, then you should do a research and get to know what he or she like doing.

Even if the two of you have nothing in common, the other person could have a skill or hobby that you may be willing to learn.

Flexibility

This refers to being able to adapt to changes positively or simply being versatile, resilient, and responsive to change. Sometimes things do not happen the way we want circumstances can occur. So, what do we do? We change our priorities to fit the situation. In business, flexibility helps the business to be successful, competitive, and to stay relevant.

Flexible people are an asset to keep in companies because they help in stabilizing situations when they strike and keep objectives achievable. They also reach out to their colleagues who may need their support.

How   to   Be   More   Flexible

- Be open-minded

  You should be ready to see things from different perspectives. You also need to listen to other people's views and be able to accommodate their opinions.

- Be optimistic

  Always stay positive no matter what changes come your way. It could be opening doors for new and exciting opportunities.

- Stay calm

  When changes happen abruptly, it can be agitating. It may bring some feelings of anxiety and stress but you need to restore calmness.

- Plan ahead

  We may not always predict the future but we can always plan for the unforeseen by measuring the risks and preparing for them.

- Have a strong network support

  Having a strong and supportive team around you is very important because no matter what challenges you go through, they will always be there to offer support. Always build a good relationship with your colleagues and family.

Good Judgment

This is the ability to weigh your options correctly. You can also say that it is the capacity to assess the situation keenly and come up with good conclusions.

Tips for Having Good Judgment

- Ask yourself if you have all the facts and if you have thought of everything else to enable you to make a judgment.

- Ask other people for their opinion about the situation you are having. This will help you gather enough information for your decision-making.

- Ask yourself if you have to make the decision now or later

- Learn from the wrong decisions that you have made in the past.

Persuasiveness

Persuasion means convincing other people to do something, to agree to a commitment or to buy a certain product. With the right training, people can learn this skill.

How to Improve Your Persuasion Skills

- Ensure that you have enough evidence for what you are saying

- Never use hesitant language like " I hope so"

- Make the other person comfortable by sitting down if they are sitting or standing if they are standing.

- Connect to your audience emotionally. Read their emotion and respond accordingly

Open-Mindedness

This refers to the ability to acknowledge ideas and opinions that are new or different from your own. Someone open-minded is flexible and adaptive to new ideas. They are always ready to change their views when given new facts and evidence.

We increase our intellectual capabilities when we learn new ways of doing things and this broadens or experiences. This can also help us in solving problems because we shall be looking at different ways of solving it. Open-minded people are interesting to interact with because:

- They are not quick to judge

- They are inquisitive about life - they want to know more about life

- Due to their flexibility to change, they are less stressed

- They have better decision making and problem-solving skills

Sense of Humor

A sense of humor gives someone the ability to perceive humor and appreciate a joke. Although some people can be born with a sense of humor, anyone can learn this skill. Humorous people are interesting and fun to be around. Research has shown that having a good sense of humor can improve your mental and physical health.

How to Develop Your Sense of Humor

- Watch stand-up comedians, read funny books, or just sit and listen to podcasts that amuses you.

- Be funny, not silly. You can always practice with the people around you.

- Learn what amuses you. If you can laugh about it, chances are someone else can also laugh about it.

- Think about timing and the audience. You cannot be funny always so do not force it to let it come naturally.

Good Manners

It refers to having good behavior and the ability to treat other people with courtesy and politeness. Some of these manners we learned them back in kindergarten and others we learn them as we grow. People with good manners are pleasant to spend time with.

How to Develop Good Manners

1. Have good conversational etiquette

    - Learn to use "please" and "thank you" words. Whenever you are requesting something, always start with the word "please." When someone does something good to you always learn to say, "thank you."

    - When meeting someone for the first time, introduce yourself by your name. For example, "Hi my name is Jane. What's yours?"

    - Listen attentively to other people when they are speaking without interrupting them.

    - Avoid using inappropriate language because they can make you sound rude.

2. Show respect to others

    - Offer to help when someone needs your help

    - Respect other people's personal space. If it does not belong to you, do not touch it.

    - Congratulate people on their accomplishments

3. Practice table manners

- Wait until everybody is served before eating

- Don't talk with food in your mouth

- Ask someone to pass things to you instead of stretching to reach it

4. Be respectful online

- Don't insult others on social media

- Avoid posting other people's photos online without their permission

- Don't overshare your personal information on social media

- Never send unsolicited messages or pictures to someone

Supportiveness

This simply means the ability to give support, sympathy, or encouragement. Having supportive people in our lives is very important because they can be a shoulder to lean on when you have problems. Supportive people are pleasant to stay with.

How You Can Be Supportive

a) Be available to listen. Sometimes talking it out and having someone to listen might be all your friend needs. Listen actively without being judgmental.

b) Be available with advice. Sometimes our friends can reach out to us for advice so give out when the demand arises.

c) Show love and affection. Let those who are around us know that we value and care for them.

d) Be that person that your friend can confide in.

e) Be trustworthy.

Be Enthusiastic

It means showing so much interest and excitement about something. This is what inspires you to put action into the task.

How to Become Enthusiastic

a) Do what you love – find what you enjoy doing

b) Think of what you want to achieve. Know your goals and how you can achieve them

c) Have a plan. Having a well-laid schedule of what you want to do will help you get enthusiastic about what you are doing

d) Surround yourself with enthusiastic people. These people will help you by encouraging you to achieve your desired goals

e) Ask questions about your abilities and ideas this will develop some enthusiasm

f) Have the right attitude

g) Give all your attention to what you are doing.

h) Lower your level of stress. Learn to control and manage stress

i) Begin whatever you want to do and avoid procrastination

Chapter 11: Influence and Leading Without Authority

Leading is a process that requires dynamic, creative, and inspiring decisions and actions, which enable people to cooperate to achieve a particular goal or ambition. Leadership is an art that requires a perfect and appropriate balancing of various leading qualities. The balance enables a person to be a leader as well as to provide direction, control, and inspiration without necessarily using authority.

Influence refers to the ability to convince someone to change his or her attitudes and behaviors in a certain way.

Having the power to influence without the need for authority is a skill, which needs an individual to master the factors that enable impact. So, how can a person exert influence and leadership without using power? Below is information regarding leadership styles, types of effects, and the conduct that one should have when leading or influencing. Read on to find out how you can effectively guide and affect the behavior of others without authority.

Leadership

It is the art of inspiring other people to accomplish a specific task. They create a vision, set a direction, and motivate others to work together as a team to realize their goals and aims. Some leaders use leadership styles to exert influence on their subordinates. They use these styles as a means of motivating or pushing people to accomplish their desired goals. Each leader has a signature style of leadership, but for producing the most effective influence, one should have a combination of them. The methods apply to different scenarios; hence, the leader can adjust their style according to the context of interest.

Democratic Style

It is a shared leadership style where the members of the group participate more actively in the processes of making decisions. The leader of the group provides control and direction while the other members actively engage and exchange ideas with each other. This style offers effective and productive leadership since the morale of the group is high, and the members contribute the best ideas or solutions. Private businesses, as well as government institutions, use it due to its engaging and effectiveness in bringing about productive results.

Visionary Style

Leaders using this style get their inspiration from looking at the bigger picture. They look at what a company can become, create a vision, and get the members to unite in working towards achieving that vision. These leaders foster tenacity and unity among the members because they tend to work best in a challenging environment. They use cohesion, confidence, and determination to work together through the uncertain or troubling times, such as during a company's transition period. Visionary leaders look to inspire innovation and help a company to move in a new and improving direction.

Commanding Style

These leaders call for immediate conformity, and it describes what most people imagine as a traditional leader. They are assertive, driven, and competitive, and get other members to work towards fulfilling their ambitious goals quickly. They are determined in their work and thus become demanding and challenging to their subordinates. They think immediately and make precise decisions, which make them the best at leading during a crisis. They are also able to work with problematic people due to their firm, domineering characteristics.

Pacesetting Style

The leaders using this style have a drive and motivation to obtain initiatives and accomplish desired results. The pacesetting leaders lead by example, where they establish high standards for both themselves and their subordinates. They identify any member who is not keeping up with the pace they set and asks them to improve. They also replace those members who fail to recover and maintain the required speed. These leaders do not have the time to give positive feedback to the employees. However, they will intervene and take over the job if the development is too slow for them.

Affiliative Style

Affiliative leaders assist in solving issues and conflicts as well as promoting harmonious interactions among group members. The leader will give a lot of praise and positive feedback to the members while encouraging them when they face a setback. They ensure that the group members relate well and feel connected by establishing emotional bonds. They use positive attitude and creativity to ensure consistent results and improving working quality. They are also honest and have clarity in their communication where they expressly state the thing they need to do and the procedure for success. They work well to resolve issues in teams with conflicts and inspire stressed members.

Coaching Style

These leaders develop the group members along with guiding them. They work in an environment where the company needs to improve its performance and results. They work to enhance the skills of the subordinates and help to prepare them for long-term strength. The employees are experienced and responsible, and they know the roles they play in the company's strategy. The leader guides them by motivating them using direction, encouragement, and inspiration. They assign the functions and duties of the subordinates while communicating openly and actively with them.

Tactics to Influence without Authority

Influencing a person is making them switch their way of thinking and acting in a way that works to accomplish an idea for the best possible outcome. It does not use force, and thus an individual needs to learn how they can exert influence without using employing authority. A few vital tactics can help a person to understand the best means of influencing others without using force. They are:

Information

A person must ensure to open a two-way path for the passing of information. One should always research, obtain information, and then share it with the other people around them. They share the knowledge that they have concisely and routinely to ensure a constant flow of updated information. The more information a leader has, the more precise instructions they can give. It enables the subordinates to understand their roles and responsibility better, and thereby responding to the directives of the leader.

Attitude

It refers to the way that an individual treats another person. Attitude determines the innate response of the audience. In turn, the reaction will decide whether they will follow the individual's lead. The approach reflects the integrity of a person and exhibiting the wrong one can make others lose trust in them. It enables a person to express himself or herself directly and honestly and boosts diligence where the person is organized and always prepared. It determines the vocal tone, choice of vocabulary, and recognition of challenging situations. The appropriate option can reflect the individual's character and increase their ability to influence.

Resources

The facilities and resources that a person has can provide essential tools for influencing other people. How an individual uses the resources that they have can determine the success or failure of an endeavor. One should use creative skills when handling them to ensure that their approaches influence others to cooperate with them. One can refer to examples from previous experiences to influence financial decisions. They can also determine the skills and procedures needed to accomplish a particular goal. They also affect people by focusing them on urgent matters and managing their workload and systems. Addressing various resources such as human and financial ones creatively and in an organized manner can allow a person to influence the group to unite and be productive.

Expertise

Credibility is an essential requirement for influence where the trust and expertise of a person make them influential. Knowledge in a specific field of interest makes other people trust the person and follow the advice or directions that they provide. People believe an expert because they think that the person is well informed with numerous experiences. Such credentials enable them to give the best possible solution to a problem, and people are responsive to influence due to their trust in their expertise.

Relationships

One should form relationships and connect deeper with others to understand their behaviors and responses. It enables a person to study the conduct, thought process, and attitudes of different people in various circumstances. The knowledge can help an individual to read and interpret a person and predict how they will respond. Foresight allows one to prepare for possible future objections by looking for other means of potentially influencing and solving problems. Relationships also create trust, which enables others to follow one's directives willingly.

How to Criticize without Being Hated

A person can ruin relationships when they use criticism carelessly. Criticism can be a tactic that someone employs accordingly and carefully, resulting in positive response and growth. Here are some of the ways that one can use to avoid hatred for criticizing:

- **Pragmatism** - This involves relating to facts rather than ideas and speculations. It is ethical to use information that one can verify, and whose accuracy relies on truths and not theoretical considerations. In some cases, when one cannot check data by facts, speculations can transform into realities by looking into them rationally.

- **Empathy** - It is the ability to identify and understand the emotions of another person. It entails giving criticism as helpful and kindly worded advice rather than harsh judgment.

- **End on a Positive Note** - At the end of the criticism, make sure group members feel good about the contributions they made or something they accomplished.

- **Follow Up** - Do a re-examination of the performance issues addressed to assess whether the problem was solved. Someone follows up assists to avoid similar pitfalls and to deal with the same challenges in the future.

- **Do Not Solve the Problem on their Behalf** - Cleaning up after group members does not encourage productivity. Instead, it harms for the reason that the problem will keep re-surfacing and will never entirely end.

- **Plan** - Planning gives the parties involved time to identify the root of the problem and time to figure out how to address it constructively.

- **Be Specific** - Be kind and direct in giving feedback. Start the criticism in a conversational style and address the issue head-on. Ask questions about the problem to provide the members with a chance to open up and confront the situation. Be open and receptive to feedback.

- **Emphasis on Improvement** - Evaluation of the individuals facilitates insightful information on their strengths and weaknesses. This emphasis leads to essential progress for both the individual and others around them.

Different Types of Influences

The type of influence that a person chooses to employ can determine whether there will be a positive or negative impact on the conduct or attitude of someone else. There are four main kinds of influence and understanding them will help an individual to know which types to adapt and which ones to avoid.

a) **Positive Influence** – A leader who uses positive influence leaves the people that he led in a better and improved state than when they initially met. They develop, connect with others, and actively lead in a way that adds value to their subordinates' lives. They use a lot of effort and energy to bring positivity and lasting success to their followers.

b) **Negative Influence** – Leading with this influence causes many damages because a person uses their power, title, or authority to force people to follow them. They have too much pride and ego and employ negative tactics to get the people to listen, support, and respect them. The resulting impact is damaging, which leads to poor performance and results.

c) **Neutral Influence** – Leaders who use this influence do not do anything to stand out from the crowd and the subordinates instead, inspire and lead themselves. They neither add nor subtract from the group that they lead because they do not actively maximize on their title or position. It is thus a type to avoid, as it is not productive.

d) **Life-Changing Influence** – it uses positive influence and years of experience to be able to exert life-changing influence. A person's words or actions are so powerful that they cause a permanent change in someone else's life. A leader with this influence uses all their effort and dedication to positively affect others and ensure they carry on succeeding even after parting ways. They sacrifice their wants and focus on improving or adding lasting value to other people's lives.

In conclusion, a person should learn how to conduct themselves and the strategies to use when they want to lead and influence without authority. Such knowledge will help them to become highly respectable leaders and exercise sufficient and productive influence on those around them.

Chapter 12: Use Storytelling to Influence People

Storytelling has been in use from time in memorial to convey messages and to influence people. Everything surrounding us has a story even our lives is a story waiting to be told! Stories are used to stimulate the audience's senses and involve them emotionally and intellectually.

A good story must have an emotional core and the characters involved should be real and relatable because it will help people to interpret the facts and see the bigger picture. For a story to be effective, you need to consider the audience, objective, and the channel to be used in advance. The story should be unique, interesting and it should have a sense of purpose, loyalty, and pride.

You can use storytelling to:

Grab Their Attention

When addressing an audience, our greatest desire is to get their full attention. However, what can you do to ensure that this is achieved? Telling a story is the best way to capture the attention of your audience regardless of their age. Here are creative ways, which can help you capture the attention of your audience:

a) Set the scene - You need to create an environment of your story by describing the environment first. Tell your audience if you are on the beach, jungle, city, countryside or in an apartment. Use enough details, which will make your audience form images or imaginations of that environment.

b) Create a killer introduction - Making the introduction of your story interesting and captivating is very crucial. This will captivate the attention of the audience since they will be eager to know what happened next and how the story ended. Just like what happened in movies, the introductory part is made to be thrilling so that you can be glued to your seat and yarn for more.

c) Create a story from your experience - You can draw stories from your real-life experiences and this will make it unique and authentic. People love to listen to real-life stories than fabricated ones and express them as if your audience were there.

d) Use movement - As a storyteller, you can move your head, hands or feet and you can even ask your audience to participate in moving some parts of their bodies during some parts of the story. This will help them to focus on what you are saying.

e) Construct anticipation - Throw questions! The story should be asking questions from the beginning and you will answer those questions along the way as you continue narrating the story.

f) Tap into your audience's emotions - Capture your audience emotionally, intellectually, and aesthetically by constructing the content of the story with the audience in mind. To grab the audience full attention, you need to provoke their emotions.

g) Use dramatic poses - When we pose during compelling moments of the story, we leave the audience in suspense. This will enable them to think critically about the story you have just given them. It will also keep them attentive up to the end of the story.

h) Change your voice with different characters - When you give the story different personalities when narrating, it makes it more interesting and memorable to the audience. For example, if you are talking about a fierce person, you can stand tall and use a deep voice to imitate them.

i) Make the character relatable - The core character of your story should be relatable to your audience by making it "feel" real. It should have its weaknesses and strengths as we all do.

j) Show creativity - Make your story interesting by having some tensions in between. Make it unique and let it sound like a fairy tale.

k) Let the story provide a solution to a problem - A good story should have a theme that will enable the audience to learn something at the end of it. It should solve a certain problem that is relatable in real life.

l) Invite interaction - At some point in the story, allow the audience to ask questions or you can ask questions and allow them to answer.

m) Make the stakes high against the goal - A story that has some painful or challenging parts should have a successful conclusion. Provide tension parts that will provoke the audience's emotions into asking whether the characters will achieve their goals. Make it hard for that hero character to achieve his/her goals.

n) Avoid diverting - Eliminate parts of the story that are not necessary and seem to divert from your objective goals.

o) Draw real-life connections - Use a real-life example to make the story more meaningful and memorable.

Engage Their Imagination

Storytelling is a powerful learning tool for both the children and the adults since it engages their imagination. A good story should engage both the intellect and imagination. The more your audience visualizes their involvement in your story, the more likely they are to take the required action. Stories that engage imagination may motivate, influence, or inspire the audience. Here are ways in which you can engage the imagination of your audience:

1. Tell a captivating story - The story can be about your personal experience, which tells the audience why you are passionate about the information you are conveying. Alternatively, you can tell the story of another well-known person, a wisdom tale or anecdote that the audience can learn from. The story should captivate your audience and it should summarize the key points of your message.

2. Ask a thought-provoking question - Although you do not expect the audience to answer the questions loudly rather silently to themselves, rhetoric questions have a persuasive effect on the audience. When designed and delivered well, the questions can influence the audience to believe in the message that the speaker is conveying. It can also arouse curiosity in the audience, and it will motivate them to want to know more.

3. Give a shocking statistic - You can use a research study done on a certain population and the shocking results to drive your point home. For example, "according to the research done on metastatic cancer by Dr. Lutz, it shows that radiation therapy provided a safe and effective relief for the patient experiencing bone pain. Therefore, radiation therapy can be advanced by using new technologies." The statistic should be directly related to your presentation. It should influence the audience to take action based on your recommendations.

4. Use a powerful quote - Make use of wise quotes that have been used by great or influential people in the world. The quote should be relevant to your message.

5. Use images or photos - It has been said that a picture is worth a thousand words. Minimize the use of text and have images instead. Image increases the understanding of the message and engages the imagination of the audience. The image metaphors in your presentation will create a brainstorming effect that will likely persuade your audience to believe in what you are trying to communicate.

6. Use a prop - Props are visual aids or objects that are used to tell a story. The audience is made to believe that the objects represent certain aspects of the story. It is used to trigger the imagination of the audience. Props can be a deck of cards, a map, juggling balls or anything that you

can use to captivate the audience's imagination. It adds humor to your story while it drives home the message.

7. Use a video - Creating videos for your storytelling can be a powerful way to connect with your audience, as they say seeing is believing. Videos evoke the emotions of your audience, get into their hearts, pain points, and desires, and give them an actionable solution.

Modulating Your Voice

This involves adjusting your voice volume to higher or lowering it to a loud whisper so that you can attract the attention of your audience. This makes your storytelling interesting since it makes it more dramatic and mysterious.

Using the same voice pitch for a long time when addressing an audience can be boring and monotonous. The audience will lose interest and withdraw their attention to something else like a phone or wandering thoughts that can distract them.

An audience can judge if a speaker is boring or not from the first few minutes of their speech. Therefore, you can use voice modulation to break the monotony, make the session interesting, and capture the attention of your audiences.

How to modulate your voice effectively:

1. Be loud and clear - Your voice should be audible enough and understandable. Someone sitting in the furthest corner should be able to get you clearly without much straining. However, this does not mean that you should shout! Shouting will only irritate your audience and they may end up losing interest or focus on what you are communicating.

2. Practice variation - Vary the tone of your voice. Using the same tone will make your audience sleep. Keep the story alive by varying the pitch and the tone of your voice. Have some parts, which you can raise your voice, and other parts, which you can whisper loudly depending on the flow of your story.

3. Emphasize keywords - When words are conveyed in the right way, they can be effective in achieving your desired goals. During storytelling, you can take some dramatic pauses to stress certain words. This will make your story interesting and interactive too.

4. Create an interesting speech for your audience - You can add humor to your story to make your audience happy. You should be able to connect with your audience through your story. Give them a story that is relatable to them by using real-life examples. Allow them to ask questions and you can ask them. Remember that your story should achieve the core goal of conveying a meaningful message

to them.

5. Make dramatic pauses - Pauses are crucial in storytelling. It creates tension in your audience, and it gives them time to reflect on what they have just heard. It leaves the audience in suspense and they will want to know what happened next. You can pause right after the introduction or when you want to introduce another part of the story.

6. You should not use the Ahs and the Uhms in your speech - The speaker should not use such fillers repeatedly when addressing an audience. This can be irritating to the audience and they might lose interest in your story or speech.

7. Sound enthusiastic and confident when delivering your speech - The audience is looking up to you to get some information. So, use an enthusiastic tone that will display your confidence. When you speak with so much confidence and enthusiasm people will take what you say seriously, and they will develop an interest in the message you are trying to convey.

Basic Rules of Storytelling

Although most storytellers are born with art, it is something that can be learned. The best way to do it is to learn from the greatest storytellers like Pixar. They are passionate about storytelling and they have won several awards for that. Although many rules have been laid down on storytelling, we shall narrow down to the very basic ones.

Here are some of the basic rules of storytelling:

It Should Have a Clear Structure and Purpose

A great way of writing an interesting story is by using the spine formula created by Kenn Adams. The formula goes like this: once upon a time, there was (________). Every day, (________). One day (______). Because of that, (______). Until finally (_____). This template is referred to as "the story spine."

The story spine has:

- A setup introduces the characters and their environment. The protagonist is introduced.

- A conflicting situation that leads the protagonist to make some decisions based on the thematic question posed by the conflict. The protagonist is subjected to some challenging situations.

- Series of intensified events based on the decision made by the protagonist in each stage of events leading to the climax.

- The climax and resolution of the conflict. The protagonist overcomes the challenges and becomes the hero.

Let your story have a purpose. What should you achieve after the end of the story? Will the audience be influenced into purchasing a product or service? There should be a goal for your story.

It Should Be Universal

You can talk about something relatable but uniquely convey the story. The best way to do this is by pulling apart stories that you like. You need to understand yourself as a writer and make good use of your strengths. Grab your most honest and unaltered perspective.

What you like from a story may not be what you like in a different story. You may like one story because of its setting and another because of its theme. Each story will "communicate to you" in a different way. Understanding what you like as an audience will help you to become a good storyteller by focusing on your strengths and working on your weaknesses.

Great Stories Have a Character to Root for (An Underdog)

People love to cheer or applaud the main character, but they also love a good underdog. Seeing the protagonist go through painful obstacles will make the audience to feel some empathy towards him/her. The more a protagonist loses, the more the audience gets devoted to his/her fate.

Every step the character moves from success towards the worst scenario, it raises the stakes and excites the audience to look forward to resolution. Your story should be able to keep the audience in that tension mood up to the moment the character overcomes the obstacles. Moreover, if the protagonist loses, the audience will feel bad.

Great Stories Should Attract Our Deepest Emotions

A good story should provoke the emotions of the audience. Try to understand how you react to stories. This will help you to come up with stories that can reach and move people. Relatable character emotions will move the audience.

It Should Be Surprising and Unexpected

Your story should not be obvious. Create tensions and suspense to provoke the audience's curiosity and emotions. For example, killing off one of the main characters in the middle of the story twists the story in an unexpected direction. The audience normally picks up the main characters from the beginning of the story and they expect them to continue to the end of the story. Therefore, when one of the main characters is eliminated from the story, it comes as a shock to the audience.

Great Stories Are Simple and Focused

A good story should be easy to understand and comprehend. Characters that portray the personalities of the protagonist should be combined to avoid redundancies in the story. You should separate the story's important parts from the unnecessary ones. Every part of your story should be relevant. The scenes and characters should fit the established tone, theme, and plot.

Include Humor in Conversation

Adding humor to the conversation makes it interesting and makes you more likable. Laughter is known to reduce stress and make our internal organs work better. It is even said that laughter prolongs your life! We may not be comedians, but we can learn to be humorous speakers to mix things up in our speech and engage our audiences. This skill can be cultivated and developed.

People like to laugh, so adding good humor to your presentation will engage the audience and make the message you are trying to convey to be memorable. Here are some tips that can help you sharpen your humor skills and add to your speech.

1. **Identify the things that make you laugh**

   Pay attention to those things that make you laugh. It could

be some TV shows, movies, or books. You can construct that style of humor that makes you laugh into your speech. Consistently watching or reading stuff that makes you laugh will ignite that feeling of being funny in you.

You can learn from standup comedians! Observe the style they use in presenting their humor. This will help you to structure and write your funny presentation.

2. Identify things that you do which makes other people laugh

We all have our inner comedian. Certain things amuse other people when we do. It could be when you yell and make fun of the things that annoy you. Pay attention to those things and think of how you can incorporate them in your speech.

3. Learn the basics of humor

If you are not lucky to be among those people who are naturally funny, you can learn some basic humor construction skills. You can construct words to create humor using several techniques and once you learn them you can easily construct your humor to add to your speech.

4. Humor comes in the rewrites

After drafting your first humor content, you can reword or add lines in funny ways and remove those lines that were not funny at all. Find the right place where you will place those touches of humor in the speech.

5. Keep working on it

Humor like any other skill requires the input of time to perfect it. You should not expect great results at the start but with your commitment, it will eventually improve. With time after practicing and learning, your speech will be funnier and even the quality will be better.

How You Can Make People Laugh at Your Sense of Humor

- **Master the language and develop a good vocabulary**

  Struggling to find the right words while trying to crack a joke can be awkward and it will end up spoiling the humor part of your speech. Enrich your vocabulary so that choice of words comes naturally, and it should be easy playing with words when trying to crack a joke.

- **Time your joke**

  You should bring your joke at the right time in your speech to make it relevant. Judge your joke to see if it would be funny now or later.

- **Control your expressions as you allow others to**

laugh

When cracking a joke, you should not burst with laughter, but you should rather hold your laughter and let the audience laugh at your joke.

- **Display confidence when cracking a joke**

Carry yourself confidently so that you can get attention. Let the humor come out naturally and say it loudly.

- **Do not try too hard to be funny let it come naturally**

You cannot force humor it should come naturally! Develop and cultivate a sense of humor before trying it out on someone else. Do not force it otherwise; it will be boring and plain.

Conclusion

Thank you for making it through to the end of *Influence Human Behavior: The Ultimate Guide to Learning the New Science Driving the Big Change. How to Win Friends and Influence People in Private Life and at Work without Authority* let's hope it was informative and able to provide you with all of the tools you need to achieve your goals whatever they may be.

After reading this book, you have discovered that manipulation seeks to change the actions or attitudes of other people using skillfully deceptive and indirect tactics; and it aims to obtain control and power over the victims by distorting their minds and exploiting them emotionally. Coercion is the use of force or threats on an individual or group of people to make them undertake or refrain from certain activities forcibly.

Jenny Cullen once stated, "I think the power of persuasion would be the greatest superpower of all time." Persuasion refers to the process of convincing someone to change their perspectives, feelings and conducts about a particular situation or person by using objective statements and arguments. Influence refers to holding the view or conception of the best possible outcome for a business or circumstance, and getting other people to work together to achieve it.

The principles of persuasion include:

- The basis of social relationships is reciprocity: if you cooperate with others, others will cooperate with you." Caroll Quigley

- The concept of scarcity uses three features to ensure effective persuasion. It uses limited offers, limited access, and loss language to form a sense of inadequacy

- The principle of authority states that people are more likely to follow the lead of someone who they consider an expert in a specific area of interest

- This principle of consistency uses the influence of active, voluntary, and public commitments to persuade someone

- The liking principle is essential in that a person that an individual likes can have the ability to influence them to act or respond in a particular manner

- The principle of consensus is where a person determines his or her conduct after studying the behaviors of other people

Becoming a good conversationalist to influence others' behavior requires having the right set of skills in one's communication toolbox. Active listening is an important aspect of conversation skills, it is the process of fully focusing on what someone else is saying, and understanding his or her meaning, instead of simply hearing his or her message.

Non-verbal communication is the process of exchanging information using body language, personal appearance, touch, gestures, postures, and proxemics. It is passing on a message by use of any other medium other than writing or speech. Negative body language occurs when we either consciously or unconscious use non-verbal communication to express negative feelings.

Emotional awareness is the measure of a person's ability to recognize and control his or her emotions, as well as other people's emotions. In other words, it is the ability to identify, understand, control, and use one's emotions in a positive way to communicate effectively, relieve stress, overcome challenges, empathize with other people, and defuse conflict.

Since reading the book is the first step, the next step is to use the tips and information you have read to influence other people positively. Of course, you will also be in a position to find out if someone else is trying to influence you in a particular way and you can choose to give in or to reject his or her attempts.

www.ingramcontent.com/pod-product-compliance
Lightning Source LLC
Chambersburg PA
CBHW061800250726

48657CB00001B/209